CW00539969

Morality in the Quran

The Greater Good of Humanity

Muhammad Abdullah Draz

Morality in the Quran

The Greater Good of Humanity

Muhammad Abdullah Draz

Revised and Edited by
Dr Basma Abdelgafar

CLARITAS
BOOKS

1 2 3 4 5 6 7 8 9 10

CLARITAS BOOKS

Bernard Street, Swansea, United Kingdom
Milpitas, California, United States

© CLARITAS BOOKS 2019

This book is in copyright. Subject to statutory exception and to the provisions of relevant collective licensing agreements, no reproduction of any part may take place without the written permission of Claritas Books.

First Published in January 2019

Typeset in Minion Pro 14/11

Morality in the Quran: The Greater Good of Humanity
By Muhammad Abdullah Draz
Edited by Basma Abdelgafar

A CIP catalogue record for this book is available from the British Library

ISBN 978-1-905837-77-9

Printed by Mega Print in Turkey

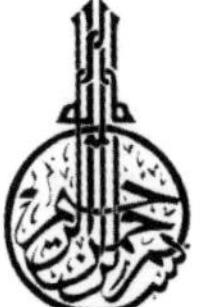

This book is dedicated to the memory of

Shaykh Muhammad Abdallah Draz

and in his words, the desire

"to promote greater understanding and enhanced humanism, in which people of good will on both sides will extend their hands for the greater good of humanity."

~ Paris, 8 June 1947

Contents

Editor's Prologue

The journey to produce this work has been truly humbling. The author, Muhammad Abdallah Draz, can only be classified as the master of the masters, a twentieth century Islamic scholar who by all measures remains in a league of his own. His theory of morality, based exclusively on Quranic teachings, has not been matched in its originality, parsimoniousness, integrity, depth and comprehensiveness by either scholars of the past or the present. Through his insight into the meanings of the Quranic text, Draz presents believers with a detailed understanding of the five critical elements of morality: obligation, responsibility, sanction, intent and inclinations, and effort. He does this while continuously emphasising the conciliatory spirit with which the text approaches what may otherwise be considered antinomies of a fundamentally religious doctrine.

I took on this project after reading Draz's doctoral dissertation, *La morale du Coran*, published in 1951. Although the thesis earned Draz an accolade of highest distinction at the Sorbonne in 1947, and its subsequent translation in Arabic in

1972 and English in 2008 garnered wide academic acclaim there is no doubt that this masterpiece has not received the global readership that it deserves. I believe that this is partly due to the complexity of the original work with its extensive references to western philosophers and comparative methodology. Draz himself had conceded "that the initial plan of this work was conceived in a much more restricted form, contemplating only the exposition of the moral law such as it emerges from the Quran and potentially from the teachings of the Prophet, who was its first authorised commentator ."[1] The demands of doctoral studies, however, required Draz to incorporate certain doctrines of the famous Islamic schools of jurisprudence as well as a number of western philosophies. The result of this comparative approach is undoubtedly brilliant and is a must read for any serious student of moral theory but it exceeds the needs and preferences of the vast majority of believers who only require a guide to what the Quran states. This effort is intended for those of us who wish to understand morality in the Quran, pure and simple. It is perhaps the most important understanding that believers must attain, aside from the primary text of the Quran.

In light of this, I have done my best to extract only what Draz would have included in his study had he pursued his initial plan. I have maintained the structure and integrity of the original work but by removing all of the comparative material. I have summarised and paraphrased much the text to make the flow and transition of his thoughts comprehensible. I have also aimed to make the text more accessible to the lay reader by simplifying some passages. This book only presents Draz's moral theory and not the latter part of that same work that discusses what he terms the practical ethics of the Quran. In that section which includes personal, family, social, state and religious ethics he avoids explanatory and comparative notes so that no effort at extraction or abbreviation is required. As such, the reader can refer directly to the original source.

A Brief on Our Esteemed Author

Muhammad Abdallah Draz was born in Egypt in 1894. He completed his religious education in Alexandria at an affiliate of Al-Azhar University. Thereafter he took up training in French to enable him to engage more fully with Egypt's independence movement from Great Britain. During the popular uprising of 1919, Draz along with a number of other young men used their communication skills with foreign embassies in the hope of convincing them to pressure Great Britain to concede to the country's demand for independence. He also used his command of French to raise awareness about the true nature of Islam.

In 1928 he joined the faculty of Al-Azhar University and in 1936 he was sent on a mission to France where he would spend the next twelve years. It was during this time that Draz produced his magnum opus on *Morality in the Quran.* In preparation for this great work, Draz would take up the study of philosophy, the history of religions, logic, sociology, psychology and ethics. He recognised that western studies would be of limited value when considering the moral theory in the Quran due to a lack of recognition of this source of knowledge. In terms of Islamic scholarship, he found that while not totally absent, the literature on morality in the Quran was sparse, incomplete or unsatisfactory.

A good deal of Draz's brilliance is due to his keen understanding and distinction between *divine law* as it applies to all humanity and *divine light* as it applies to those who choose to believe and strive to journey the path of mercy, justice and truth. The subjection of all humanity to divine law establishes a baseline of morality that gives sense to our collective existence, without which the question of disbelief would have led to chaos. Draz demonstrates that every human possesses a light that enables them to determine good and evil on a fundamental level and that propels them toward duty, kindness and charity, irrespective of faith. In contrast, the believer possesses a double light as illuminated by our nature and our assimilation of divine light. The latter proceeding from a deep knowledge, respect and incorporation of divine law into our very essence in a process that fuses our will with that of our Creator.

We must also appreciate the insight that Draz gradually attained in order to be able to present the theory of morality in the Quran. Anyone familiar with the Quranic text knows that it is not a philosophical work and is not readily amenable to theoretical modeling. Although its comprehensive nature guarantees the existence of all the elements of a moral theory, it is human knowledge and creativity that is called upon to construct the needed edifice. Through his keen knowledge of the entirety of the Quranic text and traditions of the Prophet as well as his sense of the spirit of divine law, Draz was able to perceive the defining elements of the Quranic theory of morality. These include obligation, responsibility, sanction, intention and inclinations and effort. Each element playing an indispensable role in the conscience of a believer and each requiring awareness and attention.

It is undisputable that *La morale du Koran* is a monumental achievement not only in the world of Islam but as a contribution to the literature on morality in general. That said, Draz also wrote several acclaimed books that continue to have a great impact on scholars of Islam to this day. In 1949 he was elected to the membership of *Jamiat Kibar al-Ulema*, or the association of the most senior scholars. Following his studies in France, Draz returned to Egypt to resume his academic career. In general, he preferred to keep involvement with government bodies at arms-length based on his firm belief that the integrity of religious scholarship and leadership rested on the establishment's autonomy from any government intervention. He passed away peacefully at a conference in Pakistan in 1958 at the age of 64.

Highlights from this Book

The introduction of Draz's work is simple and to the point. In it he highlights the absence of western scholarship on moral law in Islam, and its shortcomings in the Islamic literature. Regarding the latter, he asserts that works tend to be constructed from personal perspectives and that the Quran receives secondary, if any, attention. Moreover, such studies do not tend to exhibit consistent structural integrity and methodological rigor. Critiques that persist to this day.

From the very beginning we can see how the Quranic presentation of moral law serves to unify humanity. By explicitly and repeatedly stating that its word came to confirm the revelations before it, the Quran immediately establishes global respect for moral laws which preceded its revelation. The uniqueness of its message stems from its distillation of the latter from human innovations, introduction of moderation, integration of diversity and infusion of the law with a common spirit. The result is unparalleled and fulfils the promise of universalism.

This moral system guides believers in every aspect of their lives without being overbearing and unduly restricting. In fact, the absence of detailed qualitative and quantitative rules attests to the system's dependence on human reason and acknowledgement of human freedom and creativity. The Quranic system of morality approaches humanity in a holistic way, i.e., spiritually, psychologically, intellectually, logically, emotionally, physically, materially and socially. It emphasises heart and reason in an appeal to all of humanity. Each subsequent chapter is dedicated to one of the elements of the moral theory in the Quran.

In chapter one, we are introduced to the core concept of any credible theory of morality: obligation. Without obligation there can be no responsibility and without responsibility there is no meaningful conception of justice. Moral obligation is founded on human reason; a source that ensures that all of humanity strives toward a common order if only sharing a most basic understanding of moral good. Every human soul is imprinted with fundamental truths about good and evil. This is the foundation and key to our unadulterated sense of dignity. It is present in every individual irrespective of belief. Each and every normal conscience is thus gifted with a *natural* light.

Belief, however, is not dispensable. Our intellectual and emotional capabilities are not sufficient for us to navigate or even perceive everything that is right or wrong. It is necessary to resort to a higher authority beyond elements that are characterised by worldly limits. This is the role of Revelation. Divine law augments and completes our natural light. It infuses us with an auxiliary light. Thus, it is not that the unbeliever has no light, rather it is that the believer has a double source of illumination.

Reason is not, and cannot be, the author of moral law, though it remains autonomous. God is the only legislator. Whether one believes or disbelieves, the voice of conscience has only one source. If the law was not pre-established, each one of us would have the ability to change and erase the rules as he or she willed. Clearly this is not the case. What we do possess is the autonomy and freedom to adjust, accept or reject the law.

Moral law in the Quran is universally applicable to all individuals and in all circumstances. Every will is guided by abstract formulations of general rules, which includes a hierarchy of values at any given point in time and specific contexts or reality. Our conscience is available to give advice, but it is only readily so when it acknowledges, incorporates and upholds divine law. This is every believer's starting point; a position from which we exercise our full human capacity to express the law as it applies at any given moment. We become autonomous legislators beyond that initial moment of advice and recognition. We take the practice of divine law into ourselves and the world and in doing so we become embodiments of it.

Chapter two takes up the notion of responsibility which is an attendant feeling that accompanies obligation. Responsibility is comprised of judgement and action. As believers, all responsibilities are subordinated to religious responsibility. This means that any responsibility, whether personal or social, that defies sacred law must be abandoned. Thus, allegiance to God through upholding divine principles of truth, mercy, justice, equity and fairness take precedence even over our closest human relations. We are ultimately responsible and accountable to our Creator.

To be universal, moral and religious responsibility are characterised by certain conditions. The first condition is the personal nature of responsibility. Every person is solely responsible for his or her actions. The second condition is the existence of a legal foundation for responsibility. In order to be held accountable for our actions we must be knowledgeable of the law. Because moral rules are inscribed within every individual, responsibility is universally established. But responsibility toward God requires further instruction, which is provided through Revelation. Knowledge of the law, however, is not sufficient, we must be capable of receiving it and it must have been brought to our individual attention by one means or another. The third condition is associated with the internal nature of any action. In order for us to be held responsible for our actions they must be voluntary and intentional. Even more we must be free to act, this is the fourth and final condition of moral responsibility.

Freedom is associated with the efficacy of our effort. Are we in charge of our nature or is our nature in charge of us? Every person, given appropriate reflection, training and self-discipline has the power to overcome their feelings, temperaments, ideas and habits. To will something is to command it into existence. The will is therefore free in relation to internal and external acts of nature. Justice demands that such freedom or power is available to all human beings. Indeed, the human will yields only to that of its Creator, for its very existence is dependent on His Authority.

Chapter three presents the second corollary of obligation, namely, sanction. Together with responsibility this element forms the support and foundation of obligation. Sanction is the reaction of the law to our attitude. Sanctions can be classified as moral, legal or divine with each providing us with a different experience as they impact various dimensions of our reality. Moral sanction can be described as the satisfaction or remorse that we feel when we observe or neglect our duties though neither feeling is sufficient in itself. Instead, these are starting points that ought to lead to further acts of virtue or repentance respectively. Violating personal duty is considered a violation of divine rights, while violating duty toward others is considered a violation of human rights. Violating human rights can only be redressed through agreement and settlement with one's victims. If there is no opportunity for such redress in this life, then affairs will be settled in the world to come. Only errors in personal duty may be pardoned by God.

Doing good and avoiding vice have real implications for our sensibilities and higher faculties. The greater the acts of virtue that we undertake the more virtuous are the results, likewise the more we violate the law and practice vice, the weaker and more vulnerable we become. A number of Islamic practices like prayer, charity and fasting among others help believers to fortify virtuous behaviour.

Legal sanctions largely entail punishments enforced by a judicial system. Two forms of legal sanction include the *hudud* or maximum penalties and *ta'zirat* or discretionary punishments. The strict nature of the *hudud* make them minimally applicable. Instead they serve to make certain crimes extremely unattractive. Thus, while moral sanction targets our souls, legal sanction targets our physical and material existence, and thus the social order.

Divine sanction occurs at two levels for the just as well as the guilty. Retribution may be experienced in this life and/or the life to come. Rewards and punishments in this life are manifested in material, social and spiritual ways. Those in the world to come are largely expressed through descriptions of the destinies of good and evil. While spiritual and material bliss are emphasised for the former, misery and anguish are presented for the latter.

This chapter is very rich in its Quranic references. Details of a believer's practical virtues are comprehensively set out both as positive commandments and as negative duties or actions that are forbidden. Positive virtues are followed by moral praises or positive values that cannot but encourage the will to respect the law. Likewise, neglect of negative duties or transgressing what is forbidden leads to a whole host of evils that warn the will of inevitable perdition. To know, internalise and practice the virtues elaborated within this chapter is crucial for any believer. To have moral value, however, any action must be accompanied with specific and pure intentions as we learn in the following chapter.

Chapter four is concerned with examining the meanings and roles of intention and inclinations. Intention is the conscious awareness of what we are doing or are about to do. In order for an act to be morally valid it must be voluntary, conscious and intentional. Morality demands an intention. Indeed, the Quran requires the purest form of intention: virtue for virtue's sake. This is not easy to achieve. The Quran acknowledges that a believer is always working toward this ideal, we are imperfect but perfectible beings. It is our effort, not our perfection that is our saving grace.

Although the Quran consistently emphasises that the action of the heart and expressions of the body go together, it elevates the action of the heart. Good actions must spring from the depths of our hearts. Pure intention means complete submission to God. Our actions must not be influenced by our desires or external considerations including rewards or recognition. They have no moral value otherwise. Even internal actions require explicit intention. When we attempt to change something about our characters we must similarly ensure that our intentions are pure, that is, for God's sake, and not for some superficial desire. Intention therefore is always valuable. Yet the closer it comes to action, the greater its value. Every degree of effort is counted in divine justice and a well-intentioned action is better and more complete than a good intention alone.

Our inability to accurately determine our motives in every situation is not an occasion for despair. The gentleness of divine law does not require us to go beyond our abilities, while God's mercy is always present to forgive our human limits and weaknesses. Moreover, God judges every aspect of every action including all the motivations that influence our actions. Our hope is that God will grant us clemency.

Chapter five is concerned with effort, the final element of the moral theory in the Quran. Effort is our struggle with strength and perseverance. It only has value when it is directed at achieving something morally good. There are two kinds of effort that we can exert: eliminatory effort and creative effort. When we exert eliminatory effort we are resisting bad temptations. Over time the effort required to overcome temptation and achieve virtue is lessened. It is only an uphill battle in the initial phases. Our capacity to choose the good becomes gradually easier and more spontaneous over time. Once we are in control of what temps and distracts us, we must proceed to undertake what is productive and constructive. In the final analysis morality is about doing good. Thus, after eliminatory effort is creative effort. For creative effort we must act voluntarily, undertaking the best possible choice.

Nevertheless, we must do this without exhausting ourselves. The Quran exhorts us to keep our duty to God to the extent that we are capable. God does not require or accept self-inflicted suffering. Moderation is the rule. Our striving should not result in hardship but rather in justice and fairness to ourselves and those around us.

In the final chapter of this work, Draz masterfully sums up the characteristic features of the theory that he has elaborated. He explains that Quranic ethics can be qualified as religious if we identify it with its ultimate aim, or the principle which it proposes that the will adopts as the purpose of its activity. In other word, it is a uniquely religious doctrine from the point of view of intentionality. Only God can be our aim when we perform our duties, no other aim whether internal or external is legitimate. Quranic ethics constitute a religious doctrine to the extent that it is characterised by this ultimate purpose. Thus, *taqwa* or piety is its fundamental virtue.

Beyond this, however, Quranic ethics and religion cannot be superimposed and do not define each other. Quranic ethics cover everything, not only people's relationship with God. Its rules and sanction are very much verified through worldly means, i.e., moral conscience, legal power and social activism in addition to the afterlife. Moreover, it considers the demands of reason and feelings and appeals to them as opposed to basing commands exclusively on fear and hope.

Indeed, the religious element emerges only as part of a much bigger and more complex synthesis. It is dealt with as an aspect of our lives that needs order, as a means to ensure success in the application of the law, or as a justification for decisions for which we may not have the capability of determination given our human limits. Even the legislative source of the Quran is not a definite confirmation of the superimposition of Quranic ethics and religion. First, the law of the conscience existentially preceded positive religion. Second, positive law did not come to eliminate natural law and annihilate the conscience which establishes it. It is this inner authority that accepts and gives it a unique hue. Third, many duties are elaborated without quantitative details giving an active and ongoing role to the normal conscience. Every obligation rests on a calculation of our potential, realities and balance of duties. Thus, we all have a role in the legislative action necessary for determining our duty at any moment. This attests to the moderation and gentleness of duty in the Quran. The extent of our adherence is left to our individual will, creativity and aspirations. Some will be content with minimal standards, while others will soar to higher and higher heights of knowledge, awareness and action.

I am humbled and honoured to present this work, which our esteemed author hoped would serve as a "rapprochement between different cultures, to enhance understanding and humanism, in which people of good will on all sides extend their hands for the good of humankind."[2]

Basma I. Abdelgafar
Ottawa, 1 March 2018

Foreword

All praise is due to Allah alone and peace and blessings be upon His Messenger, Muhammad.

It is such an honour that I write a foreword for a book written by the teacher of teachers, Shaykh Muhammad Abdallah Draz (1312-1377H, 1894-1958CE). Shaykh Draz is one of the most important Islamic scholars of the twentieth century and we need, as a scholarly community, to exert more effort to introduce his life and works to the Muslim *Ummah* (community), especially during these pressing times. Shaykh Draz made significant contribution to the contemporary renewal of Islamic thought and jurisprudence, and he did that in a number of ways.

First, the young Shaykh Draz participated with his father, Shaykh Abdallah Draz, another prominent Azhari scholar, in the editing and commentary on Imam Al-Shatibi's seminal work, *Al-Muwafaqat*. The Drazs' edition of that book was the earliest and one of the most influential contributions to the sciences of Islamic jurisprudence and *maqasid* or objectives of the Shari'ah in the previous century.

Shaykh Draz wrote a number of important books and research articles on issues of contemporary concerns. His published research titled: *Al-Riba (Usury), Mabadi al-Qanun al-Dawli* (Principles of International Law), *and Al-Din* (The Religion)

Shaykh Draz was also the teacher of a number of significant scholars who had a major impact on Islam in the twentieth century, including Shaykh Muhammad Al-Ghazali, Shaykh Yusuf Al-Qaradawi, Dr. Aisha Abdur-Rahman (Bint Al-Shati'), Dr. Muhammad Emara, Dr. Abdul-Saboor Shahin, Dr. Fathallah Said and many others.

Shaykh Draz was nominated for the post of Grand Shaykh of Al-Azhar during the fifties of the twentieth century. He stipulated one condition before he could accept the nomination, which was for Al-Azhar to be administratively independent from the Egyptian Government. When his condition was declined by the military government at the time, he declined to accept the nomination despite repeated requests.

To me, the most significant mark that Shaykh Draz left on Islamic scholarship is his approach to the Quran. The Shaykh takes a new, holistic, integrating and systematic approach to the study of the Quran, an approach that allowed him to introduce great theories. This approach is by all means a breakthrough in the science of Quranic studies and exegesis (*tafsir*). This is evident in his tafsir of Surah Al-Baqarah, which he published under the title, *Al-Naba' Al-'Azeem* (The Great News), and is evident in this book on the moral theory of the Quran. Those reading this book will see the strength of Shaykh Draz's integrative and comprehensive approach and its great relevance to our times and beyond.

Dr. Basma Abdelgafar is introducing here a brilliant and

much needed addition to the Islamic library. May Allah reward her immensely. As detailed in her introduction, she made a synopsis/interpretation of Shaykh Draz's original research, in order to produce to the reader the Shaykhs thoughts without the long philosophical and juridical arguments he added to the academic thesis he wrote on this subject. The outcome, in my view, is a much more useful book that reveals the greatness of the theory of the Quran and the genius of the Shaykh's approach.

I would like to thank Claritas Books for this valuable addition to the contemporary literature on Islamic thought.

All praise is due to Allah alone, Lord of the Worlds.

Jasser Auda
Chairman, Maqasid Institute

Introduction

Historic State of the Matter

Moral law in Islam is a neglected area of study in western scholarship.[3] Although moral principles have been highlighted in 19th century works, these have lacked comprehensive frameworks and betrayed Quranic doctrines. Even in the Islamic literature, scholars tend to provide personal perspectives or those of their schools with the Quranic text receiving secondary if any attention. Quranic ethics have therefore been globally neglected, both on theoretical and practical levels.

The Islamic works that have attempted to analyse and present the content of the Quran have only done so partially and without robust structure or methodological rigor. Often the content of the Quran is obscured by lengthy legal commentary among other, sometimes irrelevant references. The objective of this work is therefore to explain the ethical law of the Quran as a whole and to present its principles and rules as a coherent structure independent of possible linkages with associated disciplines.

Division and Method

The Quran confirms that moral law is classified into practice and theory. With regard to the practical aspect, the Quran collates the moral laws which have been expressed previously in time and space. By purifying these laws from human discrepancies and reintroducing moderation to their core substance, the Quran serves to integrate diversity and infuse it with a common, unified spirit. In addition, the Quran provides new content to the wealth of this moral inheritance, so that the final ethical elucidation is independent, unique and original.

It is not necessary to consider all Quranic passages to establish rules of behaviour. Instead, one can follow a logical order where passages are grouped into chapters according to the type of relationship that the rule means to organise; within each category smaller groups of passages have been distinguished that are identified in such a way as to indicate the particular teaching given.

The Quran provides a comprehensive model for practical life. This includes rules on how we ought to behave within the family unit, with other people, as citizens, as communities, as nations, as well as how we ought to worship God. Rules are fixed and flexible at the same time. While providing basic order, each rule remains flexible enough to accommodate prevailing conditions of time and place and to allow for reorganisation depending on urgency.

The quest and formulation of excessive formal rules stems from a lack of trust in human ingenuity. This destructs societies and eliminates individuality and the use of reason and moral effort. In light of this, the Quran takes a moderate approach to moral legislation. While it does not quantify every rule, it does not leave matters unspecified either.

> *O you who believe, do not ask about things which, if made known to you, might harm you and if you ask about them while the Quran is being revealed they will be made known to you – Allah has pardoned these and Allah is most forgiving and forbearing. Such questions had been asked by a people before you and then they emerged on account of such as disbelievers (Al-Ma'idah 5:101-102)*

In those areas where rules are specified, flexibility in methods of application and quantity leaves ample room for intellectual, physical and moral effort on the part of individuals.

In terms of the theoretical aspect, the Quran provides all the necessary elements to construct an ethical theory though not in a unified presentation and certainly not yielding to philosophical methods and sources. It therefore supports its practical teaching with robust theoretical foundations. It informs us that the distinction between good and evil, before being a divine law, is an inner revelation, inspired to the human soul. In the final analysis, virtue takes its influence from its own nature and its intrinsic value. Therefore, Reason and Revelation are but two lights revealing the same object, a dual translation of the one single original reality, rooted at the heart of things. The Quran details the conditions and limits of human responsibility. It advises the best way to acquire virtue as well as the ultimate principle which must determine the will to act. The Quran's precision, breadth and technique are such that they naturally appeal to reasonable individuals.

CHAPTER 1

Obligation

Obligation is the core of any robust moral doctrine. Without obligation there is no responsibility and without responsibility there can be no recourse to justice. A moral rule cannot be conceived without obligation. Moral good is characterised by the imperative authority over everyone. Through this necessity everyone is compelled to carry out the same order, whatever the state of their actual feelings; a necessity which makes insubordination seem reprehensible. The Quran presents this necessity as *amr* (imperative), *kitaba* (prescription) and *farida* (duty).

Sources of Moral Obligation

Moral obligation cannot result from the uncritical acceptance of social pressure or from an impassioned aspiration toward an ideal. Instead, both of these forces must be processed by the conscience through which they attain the approval and mark of individual reason.

The Quran persistently warns against the pursuit of impetuous desire and blind conformity.[4] Both of these behaviours defy genuine morality and defeat its essential element of reason. Guarding against both these tendencies is imprinted in the primal structure of the human soul through instructions on what is good and what is evil.[5] Thus, from the very beginning human beings are endowed with moral awareness.[6] Through this awareness an individual is able to control their inclinations toward vice. Those who struggle to achieve self-control will be rewarded with Paradise.[7]

The commandment of reason is therefore the only justified rule of conduct and legitimate authority. The Quran states:

> *Do they follow the command of their reason, or is it that they are an unjust people? (Al-Jinn 72:32).*

Human beings are both legislators and subjects. This duality is confirmed by the moral experience of remorse. Our failure to undertake our duties leads to feelings of inadequacy that ought to encourage us to adjust our behaviour in order to return to our original sense of *dignity*.

The Quran continually re-awakens and re-instills within us the sense of our original *dignity*. God has dignified human beings, extended their dominion over land and seas and *favoured them greatly over many We have created*,[8] and ordered the angels to prostrate themselves before the father of mankind,[9] a title of honour of which the Quran frequently reminds us.[10] Even if we choose to overlook the outer signs of human dignity, and consider them from the point of view of their moral value, we find that the Quran considers human nature to be intrinsically good. *The human being was created in the finest mould*.[11] Only those who do not believe and do not practice good works have an unsettled and unbalanced nature[12] and that *fall lower than the lowest of creatures;*[13] only those who *have a heart and do not think, eyes and do not see, ears and do not hear* make themselves *brute beasts or worse.*[14] It is thus a matter of free temporal choice. Everything resides in the good or bad use that we make of our superior faculties. Cultivating these faculties *ennobles the soul*; forsaking them *darkens it.*[15]

The appeal to feelings in the Quran, only occurs under the guidance of reason, which can assess the benefits and harms of acts and prioritise values. It therefore sensitises us to certain feelings that are necessary for upholding moral order. Human kinship, for example, is presented as the principle upon which all social duties are based.[16] In light of this, the slanderer is compared to "someone who *would like to eat his brother's dead flesh,*" adding "*you would detest it.*"[17]

The focus on reason, however, does not mean that we have the intellectual and emotional means to distinguish between all that is right and wrong. Human intelligence is not omnipotent and therefore is subject to fallibility. Beyond certain essential duties, acknowledged by every normal conscience, *moral certainty must gradually give way to conjectures, hesitation and aberrations.* The diversity of human perspectives on an infinite number of issues demonstrates that intelligence and feelings are necessary but insufficient factors in the determination of moral behaviour. To stop at these two factors then leads us to an unresolvable predicament of whose law ought to apply in any given situation.

When considering morality, we must resort to a higher authority beyond society. Only God, the Creator of the human soul, fully knows the laws of its advancement and success.[18] *It may be that you hate something when it is good for you and it may be that you love something when it is bad for you and Allah knows and you do not know* (2:216). Recourse to divine reason is therefore a necessity. Only Revealed light can assist innate light; only divine law can continue and complete natural moral law. The believer thus has two sources of illumination whereas the unbeliever only one.[19]

It is important to recognise that this does not translate into two separate sources of moral obligation but rather one with two tiers. It is our reason which enables us to heed divine reason. The suggestions given by our conscience only have moral worth to the extent that we believe them to represent moral truth and not emotional impulses no matter how serious. All our efforts of reflection have the aim of deciphering this truth, which is innately imprinted within us. In essence, the autonomy that is attributed to our reason means that we are our own legislators. This, however, does not mean that reason is the author of the law since that would allow it to change the law as it pleased. The inability to do precisely this means that the law is pre-established and embedded within each individual in such a way that it cannot be erased.

To listen to reason is to listen to God's voice whether or not we acknowledge it as such. Natural and revealed light emanate from a single source. It is always God who specifies our duty. God is the only legislator in this sense.[20] The Quran is the primary and ultimate source for understanding of God's will. Even so, it does not present divine commandment as absolute power but rather provides justifications for its rules. Thus to make amends with our neighbours is supported by the maxim, "reconciliation is better."[21] Likewise to practice fair trade is justified with the statement, "that is beneficial and gives the best result."[22] When asking men to lower their gaze and master their senses, the Quran tells us, "that is purer for them"[23] and so on.[24]

The intrinsic value of moral action remains the essence of duty. Rules are justified through values in an appeal to human reason: it is therefore in the notion of value that the true source of obligation resides. The essence of what is just and good, however, can only ever be partially detected with human capabilities. The believer resorts to divine reason to direct them toward perfect morality.

The Characteristics of Moral Obligation

Moral law, like all other types of law, must by definition be applicable universally. The Quran addresses all of humanity.[25] As it is applied to oneself, it is applied to others,[26] to one's kin as it is to strangers, to the rich as it is to the poor,[27] outside of the community as it is inside;[28] whether it concerns a friend or an enemy.[29]

Universality is not only expressed in terms of extent of coverage but also as it applies to the diversity of circumstances that each individual inevitably faces. Given these natural states, each duty is only commanded to the furthest practical extent, without yielding to subjective states or personal interests. The Quran reveals that cynics only obey the law to the extent that they profit from conformance, while believers accept it unconditionally.[30] In light of this, values such as generosity are commended in times of ease and hardship,[31] and courage is expected to brave hunger, thirst and fatigue.[32] Those who shun generosity and valour on account of fear of life's hardships are reprimanded in the Quran.[33] True believers have no choice when divine law is decreed.[34]

Moral law supposes freedom of choice regarding respect or violation of the law. Choice is *de facto*, not *de jure*, since the law has been pre-established. The Quran consistently stresses this point for the duty of faith as well as practical virtue.[35] Moral obligation thus imposes itself on the will as something which must be. In other words, it acts on our conscience. Free and voluntary agents must perceive the value of duty as worthy of attainment. The freedom to choose gives us feelings of power, while its consequences entails subordination or duty. These are the characteristics of all laws.

Moral law requires action for its own sake because of its inherent value. An action must be obligatory or good in itself without regard for consequence. From the legislative perspective, the Quran's approach to ethics is progressive. The legislator can justify his orders but this is not strictly a moral role. It is performed to educate using a form of gradualism that may be effective for beginners. Morality, however, becomes self-supporting as learning advances.

From the practical perspective, moral action consists of physical deeds that must always be conscious, voluntary, and intentional. In other words, morality requires an underlying spirit. An action that does not conform to these characteristics may be legal but it does not hold moral value. The law of duty is characterised by the fact that it is a law of *freedom* and reason, of *intrinsic* value and is essentially *spiritual* in its activity. The practice of moral law is thus conditioned by human nature, the realities of life and the hierarchy of action.

A. Possibility of Action

Possibility of action is a fundamental condition of moral obligation. The Quran states:

> *Allah does not oblige any soul except to the extent that He has given it (Al-Talaq 65:7)*

We do not oblige any soul beyond its capacity (Al-An'am 6:152; Al-Mu'minun 23:62)

Allah does not oblige any soul beyond its capacity (Al-Baqarah 2:286)

Those states of the soul that do not submit to the will are not objects of moral obligation. Emotional and involuntary states, however, can be acquired through voluntary actions. The Prophet said: 'forgive one another (or shake hands) and your resentments will disappear; exchange presents, so as to foster mutual friendship.'[36] These are voluntary actions that give rise to love. In contrast, the Prophet also cautioned against the consequences of anger. He said 'do not become irritated or angry' to avoid the outcomes of these behaviours.[37] To ward off anger, the Prophet suggested the performance of ablution, i.e., using water to soothe emotions and calm down. He also recommended changing body posture.

Because emotions and other involuntary states can be subject to our power of action and rational calculations (albeit indirectly), to cause or avoid them, they remain within the realm of obligation. All impossible acts are eliminated as these do not accord with divine justice and wisdom.

B. Gentle Practice

Far from demanding the impossible, Islamic ethics tends toward ease and endurance. In this regard the Quran states:

Allah desires ease for you, He does not desire difficulty for you (Al-Baqarah 2:185)

> *He has chosen you and not placed any discomfiture in your religion* (Al-Hajj 22:78)

> *Allah desires to lighten matters for you, and man was created weak (Al-Nisa' 4:28)*

> *And we have not sent you except as a mercy to the worlds (Al-Anbiya 21:107)*

Thus, our capacity to bear what is demanded of us is a hallmark of Islamic ethics. This is why we are warned against excessiveness even in acts of piety where the conditions of our lives may limit our abilities.[38] Life's circumstances may affect consistency and in some cases present insurmountable challenges even when it is our ardent desire to undertake certain acts. Each individual must also tend to their own needs and those of others in the course of their daily lives, which may also impact the time available for pure acts of worship.

These exigencies emerge as a blessing since they prevent believers from performing acts mechanically. Every act of worship must be performed with reflection.[39] Also, acts must not become so tiresome or burdensome that they no longer serve to elevate the spirit. This risks abandonment altogether.

Gentleness does not change the structure of action but rather its timing. To voluntarily stop, or spread acts over a reasonable duration of time ensures longevity of performance. It is clear that duty in the Islamic moral order is conditioned by circumstances since 'normal' conditions are not always the norm. Mercy demands appropriate modifications when the circumstances of life change. The changes to duty can be temporary or permanent, general or specific, complete or partial regarding both actions and people.

Gentleness is also prescribed when changing a bad habit. Thus the prohibition of alcohol was affected in four stages. The first stage establishes the good that God provided through the fruit of the date-palm and the grape-vine[40] followed immediately by the possible derivation of intoxicants and wholesome provision.[41] The existence of a potential harm does not negate the value and use of the original good. In the second stage the Quran tells us that the harm of alcohol and games of chance is greater than the benefit[42] thereby raising awareness of the nature of both acts without making a definitive statement. In the third stage, believers are exhorted to avoid prayer when they are in a state of intoxication.[43] With obligatory prayers occurring five times a day and spread over the course of our waking hours, drinking becomes even more challenging and less likely. Finally, an ultimate prohibition is instituted when the Quran states that intoxicants and gambling are idolatrous practices and must be abandoned by believers who wish to prosper.[44] Gradualism and progressivism are the Islamic approach to changing harmful habits.

The Quran itself was revealed over roughly two periods lasting about a decade each. In the first span, principles and general rules of behaviour were established. In the second, practical rules and application were the focus. New duties were separated by significant intervals allowing individuals and the emerging community to internalise and adjust to the Islamic moral code. This legislative wisdom of gradualism is justified as follows:

> *It is so that We may secure your heart by it (Al-Furqan 25:32)*

And it is a Quran which We have portioned, so you can recite it to people in stages (Al-Isra 17:106)

This approach is particularly relevant in the political arena where decisions impact the public at large. Truthful, yet unpopular decisions, have a greater possibility of wholesale rejection if they are introduced instantaneously and comprehensively.

C. Delimitation and Grading of Duties

Every individual is a synthesis of relationships including the personal, familial, social, human and divine. This system of elements is interdependent, tightly integrated, and subject to evolution and progress, so that no element can be neglected without damaging the admirable proportion in which the individual is created. The vast majority of people define duty toward and within these relationships according to a minimum standard. Yet, beyond this minimum their remains *creative, constructive virtue*, a field of activity which is so vast that it comprises endless *degrees, all possible and practicable*. Those with higher capacities and sense of morality will tend to equate goodness with duty rendering minimal standards unacceptable for leading a fulfilling life.

This high degree of moral sense is not to be expected of everyone. Rather, each individual must undertake a combination of duties that ensures the maintenance of the diverse relations of which they are part. Such contribution serves not only to elevate the subjects of duty but also to preserve the bearer himself. Thus, we must partake in all values before we choose to specialise in one, or several, more than others.

Duty only occupies a certain part of what is good leaving space for us to satisfy other needs. The realm of good has mandatory minimums as well as more meritorious and open increments. The intelligence and conditions of every individual will determine its tendencies in this regard. Recognition of this subjectivity means that strict duty toward others is largely defined and accomplished in the negative sense, i.e., not to violate others. People are therefore entitled to our justice but not to our charity. From this perspective, selfishness becomes enshrined in law.

To rectify this, Islam seeks to present people with two alternatives on a continuous spectrum: from obligatory good to the recommended good. The obligatory good allows for suitable participation in that which is meritorious, while the recommended good exhorts us to ever higher refinements of our contributions.[45] Above the strict obligation, it places the virtue of tolerance and generosity.[46] As examples, the Quran states: if a debtor cannot repay his debt, more time must be given but debt forgiveness is recommended;[47] it is a right to demand justice but to forgive and overlook is better;[48] to perform one's duty well is good but to do good spontaneously is praiseworthy with God.[49]

The hierarchy of values in the Quran is not limited to an elaboration of positive as well as negative values. It also elaborates a non-value between the value and anti-value: a non-proscribed between the prescribed and proscribed. Prescribed acts are distinguished as primary duties, then other obligations and then more meritorious acts. Proscribed acts are presented as unforgivable, then bad, then serious or pardonable. Non-proscribed acts are permissible and tolerated. Permissible acts are morally neutral, i.e., choosing between two or more equally lawful alternatives. Allowances are subject to spatial and temporal determinations. The rule, however, is not subject to the situation rather we must adjust to situations that are beyond our control without altering the integrity of the rule. When obstacles become insurmountable, obligations give way to necessity. The aim of gentleness of this legislation is therefore not to diminish, but to rationalise effort.

Antinomies of Obligation

The notion of obligation forces us to consider a number of practical antinomies. The two considered in this work are unity and diversity; and authority and liberty.

A. Unity and Diversity

The scientific nature of ethics requires that its laws are both necessary and universal. But because it is also a normative science that governs human behaviour, it must also consider the realities of life which are characterised by change, diversity and renewal. Striking a balance between these two extremes is the first ethical challenge.

B. Authority and Liberty

The second ethical challenge, related to the first, involves resolution of the opposing tendencies of the authority of the *legislator* and the freedom of the *subject*. Robust authority requires consistent and definitive rules so that circumstances do not alter them. In this sense moral law is no different than natural law. Freedom and the application of our conscience under such circumstances, however, are pointless. Yet, if complete freedom of action is accepted then rules emerge as nothing more than advice which can be accepted or ignored according to our impulses. The Quran takes a conciliatory approach to these assumed contradictory demands.

Quranic Conciliation

The ideal of Quranic ethics is to perform one's duty without being concerned about the moral good at which it aims. Instead, we evaluate actions in relation to the idea of a general rule which is applicable irrespective of consequences, moods and emotions.

The rule of our own behaviour is measured against that with which we demand of others. The Quran states:

> *Do not give away the meanest of your earnings [things] that you yourself would not take except while cringing (~Al-Baqarah 2:267).*

Similarly, the Prophet stated 'nobody can call himself a believer if he does not like for his brother that which he likes for himself.'[50] Thus, we accept the reciprocity and universality of duty.

An important realisation emerges from this behavioural rule: when a law is established as just it ought to be universalised. The emphasis here is not on the possibility of universalisation but rather on the notion of justice. The rule must first and foremost be just. Undoubtedly there are many rules that can be universalised to various extents but which do not exhibit such moral necessity. Necessity is the justification for universality. Moral necessity proceeds from an internal value. For example, we strive for universal peace because it is necessary for human well-being and existence.

Universality is distinguished according to degrees. We cannot credibly grant all duties the same importance or urgency. The extension of any duty can only be determined through an understanding of the functions of its constitutive elements as well as the realities of prevailing conditions.

Without such an application of division and definition of duties, what is initially considered a duty may result in a harm or more seriously a crime.

Although many duties are not opposed to one another, that is, do not compete in their practical application, many others do. Thus, the duty not to lie or to kill can always be undertaken simultaneously. However, the duty to tell the truth while desiring to be polite, or to protect a third party requires a moral determination that defines and prioritises one imperative over the other. A hierarchy of values is consistently constructed and reconstructed in accordance with a set of perceived parameters and their impact on our relationships. In other words, our hierarchy of values always remains dynamic and flexible. That which is deemed necessary in one case may be secondary in another and irrelevant in a third.

Our wills are guided by abstract formulations of general rules and particularities of specific situations. Only reality can dictate the ultimate hierarchy of values. In this way, in order to determine the duty of a given moment, the last word will be reserved for each person's own judgement, maybe even to what is called their *sixth sense*.

Conclusion

In the Quran we are neither told to adhere to what seems good to us, or to some inflexible set of rules. It states: *be mindful of Allah, as much as you can* (64:16). Obligation is thus defined in accordance to the ideal while allowing full account of our realities. It is at one and the same time *submission to the law and freedom of the self*. Only the conscience of a believer can internalise this balance without contradiction since it accepts positive teachings where duties are defined and ranked while recognising the sanctity of a lived reality.

The believer's conscience incorporates within itself the authority of the legislator, who is always present to give advice. It, therefore, cannot undertake acts that defy the author of the law without betraying its very essence. In doubtful situations, which are a consequence of the human condition and of the freedom granted by this condition, it is essential to try to understand divine recommendation considering the entirety of all rules. Should this effort be undertaken in earnest, there is no guilt on the believer should the solution turn out to be less than optimal.[51] The Prophet elaborated on this principle by stating the following:

> *The permissible and the prohibited have been made clear; but between the two are unclear cases. He who restrains himself when in doubt preserves his faith and honour.*[52]

> *Avoid that which throws you into doubt; choose that which does not trouble you; truth is peace; falsehood leads to suspicion.*[53]

> *Ask your heart, consult your conscience; good is what gives peace to the soul and the heart; evil is that which troubles the soul and makes the heart palpitate, whatever people may say and whatever they may offer you.*[54]

Even when the law is not doubtful, the conscience still has a role to play in the application of duties. Since there are many ways to understand a rule, apply it and reconcile it with other rules, our individual imprint on each act remains pivotal. Moreover, all acts are characterised by numerous distinctive features that cannot be fully considered. Effort is required to appreciate values and address them.

Conforming one's duty to objective reality is a universal duty. Every person must ask themselves if the action they intend to undertake satisfies the rules. This indetermination is the most eloquent solicitation addressed to our conscience to continue the legislative work which the law has begun. We engage in this process until we are satisfied with our duties and their associated actions. This is the realm in which the authority of the law ceases and our liberties begin.

It is clear that rules are not meant to obstruct freedoms but to enhance them by giving us a starting point. The value of these points of departure is clarified when we consider the variety and quantity of moral precepts that we must manage and prioritise at any given moment given our finite capacities. This system is both efficient, in terms of conserving time and energy, and effective, in terms of reducing the chance of errors. To illustrate consider the following:

My body, my mind, my family, my homeland, each of my attachments requires an action determined by a rule. However, when I get up in the morning, I organise a timetable of tasks in different ways and set out the itinerary in order to put them into action. During the given lapse of time, I can integrate a number of diverse good works, perform one to a higher degree of perfection than the others, accomplish one as early or as late as possible, content myself with ordinary forms of doing good or strive to create something new, of greater value. In such a way everyone may freely compose an original *page* of their moral life, whilst respecting the *general rules* of this human art.

The rules have already been implicitly or explicitly made by the Legislator. However, it is we who define our concrete duties from these ideals to the best of our capacity. True morality is thus akin to citizenship: *participating in some way in the authority of the law, by the choice and initiative to which we are entitled.* From this perspective, true morality is both pure submission and absolute invention. By adhering to the sacred law, our conscience assimilates it, defends it, makes it its own, as if it participated in the creation of eternal truths. When we synthesise different rules, adjusting them to our situation, we do not do so in the absence of a master, but under his patronage, his supervision and control. We always draw inspiration from him, as if he still continued within us the role of legislator, down to the slightest detail. From this one can say that here, between the agent and the author of the law, there is not only collaboration but union. One could say *a fusion of two wills.*

CHAPTER 2

Responsibility

The notion of obligation gives rise to two corollaries, responsibility and sanction. They are respectively the support and foundation of obligation. To be obliged is to feel some level of responsibility, which must somehow be reinforced by appropriate sanction;

> *"To be responsible is to be obliged to answer for something, to be accountable to someone."*

This chapter considers the general characteristics of responsibility, as well as its conditions from moral and religious perspectives and finally its social dimension.

Analysis of the General Idea of Responsibility

Responsibility is characterised by both action and judgment. By exercising our judgment, the notion of responsibility legitimises an action prior to its performance. Thus, the first step is to take something upon ourselves, and then employ our capacities to realise it. The Quran alludes to the latent acceptance of responsibility by human beings:

> *We offered the Trust [moral law] to the heavens, the earth and the mountains, but they refused to bear it and shrank from it. But the human being bore it. Indeed, he [the human being] was unjust and ignorant (Al-Ahzab 33:72)*

This is only a latent aspect, an aptitude which hardly assumes responsibility in an *action*. The latter will only happen when certain conditions (pertaining to age and health, for instance) have been realised, so that our promises and our engagements are given moral significance. It is not even sufficient that these general conditions have been brought together for us to become effectively responsible. Concrete circumstances must also be added and invite us to insert our activity within the web of facts. It is true that we are never without such circumstances: all of us necessarily maintain some sort of connection, occupy a certain place and exercise some function within society. Even when alone and isolated, we are responsible for the purity of our heart and righteousness of our thoughts, as well as the protection of our life and health. It may, therefore, be maintained that some degree of responsibility is attached to human life at every moment, which is not only virtual, but also real and present. As soon as the general conditions exist, the variety of situations occurring only serve to specify and define the object of this responsibility. We are naturally responsible before becoming or being made morally responsible.

When we intervene of our own initiative to accept, change, or modify a particular possibility, we become the authors of our choice. *Responsibility* becomes *imputably*. The first moment of responsibility thus inspires in us a feeling of power. This is a *force*. In the second, by contrast, we take on an attitude of humility and submission. This is a *duty*.

The assumption of an obligatory act focuses our attention on two dimensions of responsibility. The first considers the completion of the act and the second its judgment. Judgment can proceed from within us, as when we impose obligations on ourselves or from the outside as when obligations are determined by society or a higher authority, i.e., God. This gives rise to three types of responsibility, purely moral, social and religious. In this regard the Quran states:

> *Believers, do not betray Allah and the Messenger, or knowingly betray others [by committing an abuse of a trust] (Al-Anfal 8:27).*

The Quran presents religious responsibility as purely moral responsibility since any responsibility enters the moral realm when it is accepted by our persons. The Quran often reminds people to honour their pledge of faith and all its associated commandments.[55]

In Quranic ethics any responsibility, both personal and social, is subordinated to religious responsibility, i.e., must be divinely approved. All responsibilities emanating from personal initiative, that do not violate the law, must be honoured:

> *Honour your contracts; your contracts will be asked about (Al-Isra 17:34).*

Responsibilities that may violate the law have to be abandoned. The Prophet said: 'Whoever has vowed to perform a pious duty must do so; but whoever vows to commit a sin must abstain.'[56] He also said: 'Muslims always keep to the provisions of their contracts.'[57] Thus, 'any stipulation not legitimated by God's Book is null and void.'[58] In a similar vein, 'any arrangement which aims to establish harmony between Muslims is valid, as long as it does not prohibit something that God has allowed, or allow something which he has prohibited.'[59]

The same applies for our social responsibilities where not even the closest blood relations excuse a believer from upholding justice. The Quran states:

> *O you who believe, establish equity, witness for Allah, even if it is against yourselves, your parents, or your close relatives (Al-Nisa 4:135).*

It follows that obedience to leaders and superiors is also subject to divine law.[60] In cases of dispute, the Quran and Sunnah must be consulted;[61] any violations must be rejected.[62] The Prophet clearly states, 'There is no obedience to the created when it means disobeying the Creator.'[63]

When there is harmony among personal and social duties with Islamic rules, we become morally, socially and religiously responsible subjects. Nevertheless, each realm retains its specificities and conditions. Moral responsibility is exercised immediately and in a permanent way, social responsibility functions only intermittently, and religious responsibility only appears clearly on the day of the day of judgment. Moreover, Islamic legislation does not place similar importance on the conditions which establish our moral and religious responsibility in comparison with our social responsibility. General conditions of moral and religious responsibility in the Quran extends to all creatures endowed with reason. Thus, we read:

> *There is no one in the heavens and earth but who will come to the All-Merciful as a servant (Maryam 19:93)*

> *So by your Lord, We will question them all, about what they used to do (Al-Hijr 15:92-3)*

> *Most certainly We will question those to whom the Messengers were sent, and we will question the Messengers (Al-A'raf 7:6)*

On the Day of Judgment we will be questioned concerning our moral responsibility.[64] All acts will be revealed,[65] whether hidden or manifest.[66] Even our faculties will be questioned, bearing witness as to how we employed them.[67] Specifically, the Prophet said that everyone will be questioned regarding, 'in what occupation he spent his life, for what motive he acted, from what source he made his fortune and how he used it, and how he used his own body.'[68] In other words, everyone will be questioned with regard to their trusts.[69]

In order to be universal, however, moral and religious responsibility express certain conditions that are detailed in the Quran. This is the subject of what follows.

Conditions of Moral and Religious Resposibility

a. The Personal Nature of Responsibility

The personal characteristic of moral and religious responsibility is a fundamental principle in the Quran. In addition to innumerable other proofs, the following verses clearly make this point:

> *For it [the soul] is what it has earned; against it, what it has acquired (Al-Baqarah 2:286)*

> *And whoever accrues a bad deed, he only accrues it against his own soul (Al-Nisa 4:111)*

> *Whoever is guided is only guided for his own soul and whoever is misguided is only misguided to his detriment and no soul will bear another's burden (Al-Isra 17:15)*

> *Fear a day when no parent will be able to atone for his child, or child for his parent (Luqman 31:33)*

> *This day every soul will receive its desert for what it has earned. No injustice will there be on this day for Allah is swift in account (Al-Mu'min 40:17)*

> *And for all are degrees in accordance with what each did (Al-Ahqaf 46:19)*

> *And that there is naught for man except what he strove for (Al-Najm 53:39)*

Every person is therefore responsible for his or her actions. No blame or praise can be reassigned to anyone else.[70]

Adam's sin in the Quran was due to an accidental weakness; an act of forgetfulness that resulted in a lapse of responsibility. His recognition of having sinned and demonstration of repentance was sufficient for his reinstatement among the ranks of the guided.[71] Human nature is generally described as follows in the Quran:

> *Surely, We created man in the best form. Then We reduced him to the lowest of the low, with exception to those who believe and work righteousness, they will have a joyful remuneration. (Al-Tin 95:4-6)*

Only the guilty party can redeem themselves in Islam. No innocent soul can be sacrificed in another's place. This is against divine justice, and indeed that of human sensibilities.[72]

Two exceptions appear to be made to individual responsibility in the Quran. In the first instance we read:

> *They will bear their own burdens and other burdens together with their own (Al-Ankabut 29:13).*

And in another we are told that the children of the faithful will be treated equally to their ancestors provided that they follow them in faith.[73] The first exception is moderated as follows:

- There is never mention of total transfer of blame or praise. In fact, personal responsibility remains intact.
- It is only a supplementary act of blame or praise.
- As for the guilty, the Quran further stipulates that they were actively engaged in destructing and misleading other people.[74] Thus, they are responsible for the wrong that they willfully instigated.
- This does not exonerate those who follow them. The Quran presents this in the form of blame laying on the Day of Judgment where the weak will blame the

strong. Both parties will ultimately be held to account in accordance with their participation.[75]

- Where there is no causality or mediation each individual remains personally responsible.

Thus, people are responsible for the consequences of their behaviour through time and space whether what they undertake is good or reprehensible. The Prophet had said:

> 'Death ends all human actions except in three cases: a continuous charity, valuable knowledge, or descent offspring.'[76]

Thus, even after our death, the consequences of our intentional actions continue to accumulate in our balance of deeds as confirmed by the Prophet.[77] In conformity, any murder committed unjustly will be partly charged against its first perpetrator.[78]

In addition to responsibility for positive sin, individuals are also responsible for complacency toward bad conduct. Injustice and wrong-doing must be challenged and prevented by all open legal means and by employing all of our capabilities. People in ancient times were repeatedly admonished for not opposing the reprehensible behaviour of those among them.[79]

We must not confuse this with collective responsibility. Collectivity in Islam is the sum of individual consciences who are aware of the moral rule, what has violated it, but who allow criminals to thrive and continue unabated with their destructive practices. Those who make an effort to rectify the situation are redeemed.[80]

As for the second exception to personal responsibility,

namely, the future equality between believers and their offspring, the issue appears to be a misunderstanding of the Quranic verse. The text only alludes to a reunion between believers and their faithful offspring and not as an overture of equality. It is solely a promise of uniting people with a similar affinity to faith. Within this heavenly congregation, however, individuals will nevertheless be accorded their deserved station in keeping with their deeds.

Finally, there is no contradiction with the concept of *shafa'a* or intercession of the angels and prophets in favour of the just, with the permission of God. Intercession must satisfy three conditions: God's permission; God's approval of the subject of intercession; and, only truth about the good deeds of the subject can be spoken in support of their salvation. Thus, our efforts, prayers and future intercession, if we are permitted such a role, only serve to reveal what ought to be so in accordance with God and His laws. It is ultimately the truth of every individual that matters and that can be accounted for. No intercession can introduce false support for any soul. Each soul will be judged according to its own merits.

Our actions must be in conscious harmony with the law to attain praise. Such consciousness dwells in our hearts.[81] As a result, we are not equipped to judge others as God will judge them. Nor can we fully grasp how we, ourselves, will be held to account. However, this is does not diminish from the necessity of our self-judgment. Not knowing the exact details does not change anything of the matter of individual responsibility, and its unique basis for moral merit and all ensuing rewards.

God's mercy encompasses all creation.[82] It is in virtue of this that everyone has the moral and material means to understand the law and obey it. There is a portion, however, reserved for those who piously observe their obligations. The Quran states:

> *The most dignified among you with Allah is the most heedful (Al-Hujarat 49:13).*

B. *Legal Foundation*

No one will have to account for his actions without having been informed of the rules first. Information is provided internally and externally. Moral rules that are inscribed within us, that is, those which yield to our natural faculties can be considered universal. Everyone is privileged in this way, so that responsibility is universally established within a common framework.

This is insufficient to establish our responsibility toward God, which demands particular and explicit instruction. Thus, we read in the Quran:

> *And it is not for Allah to misguide a people after guiding them until He had revealed to them what they should heed (Al-Tawbah 9:115)*

> *Nor do We chastise until we have sent a Messenger (Al-Isra 17:15)*

> *And your Lord never destroyed towns without first sending to its core a Messenger to recite Our Signs to them (Al-Qasas 28:59)*

This principle of education is justified by God's grace to protect man from using his reason to reject God.[83] The preoccupations of daily life combined with weakness in our moral will obscure our inherent light. In recognition of these two realities, and to alleviate their influence on our moral development, God has strengthened our natural light with that of Revelation.[84] Thus, God has made it an obligation upon Himself to instruct men before calling them to account.[85]

The existence of laws is not enough, nor is providing messengers to proclaim them. The teaching must reach men and they must be capable of awareness. Three categories of people are therefore exempt from responsibility: the sleeping until they wake, the insane until they are cured, and children until they mature.[86] The last of these does not preclude children from being taught responsibility, but rather it emphasises the responsibility of those who care for them as well as those who influence the environments with which they live.

Therefore, the law has to be made available, one must be in the correct state to receive it and it must have been brought to one's personal attention for the conditions of responsibility to be satisfied.

> *This Quran has been revealed to me so that I may warn you by it, and whomsoever it reaches (Al-An'am 6:19)*

Moreover, one must be in a state of remembrance from the perspective of divine justice. Forgetfulness is a natural phenomenon which does not result from an intentional act or personal fault. So long as we mend our ways when we realise our mistake, we are not responsible. Thus we pray:

> *O Lord, do not take us to task if we forget (Al-Baqarah 2:286);*

to which the Prophet assured, 'God said: Yes, I have promised.'[87]

C. The Internal Aspect of an Action

Our relationship with the law is one of knowledge, that with action is of the will. Our conscience holds this dual relationship simultaneously. We may know the law but decide not to conform. All involuntary action is removed from the realm of responsibility. In Quranic terms it does not constitute something the soul has earned.[88]

In order for us to be morally responsible for an action, that is, for it to warrant merit or blame, we must perceive of the action in the same way as the legislator. Morally, there is no obedience or disobedience unless there is complete correspondence between the action as it was commanded or forbidden and the action as it was performed. For example, to kill a person instead of an animal target. The intention of the voluntary act was not to kill a human. One cannot be held morally responsible under such circumstances.

> *Allah will not take you to account for the literal expressions of your oaths but He will take you to account for what is in your hearts (Al-Baqarah 2:225)*

This demonstrates that the act must be voluntary and deliberate to warrant moral responsibility.[89] Both the natural and moral qualities of an action have to be intentional. Good faith can only be determined through an appreciation of sincerity and insincerity.

Sincerity of intention ensures that we do not develop secondary intentions which are premeditated justifications to obscure another deeper intention. The secondary intention does not absolve from moral responsibility. If I am convinced wholeheartedly that I am not violating the law, there can be no reproach even if my actions are misguided. The Quran states:

> *Your Lord is better acquainted with what is in your inner selves. If you are righteous, then He is toward those who turn to him Forgiving. (Al-Isra 17:25)*

Intention must be complete, that is, the will envisages not only the natural characteristics of its objects, but also its moral characteristics as they have been conceived by the Legislator. Any divergence is deemed an involuntary error. The Quran states:

> *And there is no blame on you in what you mistook but only for the deliberateness in your hearts.*[90] *(Al-Ahzab 33:5)*

Action has moral value if it is performed with the intent or will to obey the law. Likewise, reprehensible acts do not entail responsibility if they were unintentional, in spite of the law. The reverse, however, is not true. Good intention does not mean that its object is moral. Intentionality is thus a necessary condition for responsibility and morality but it is also insufficient. We have thus far covered knowledge, will and action.

D. Freedom

The will may be occupied by other forces which influence choice. We must therefore examine the extent of our *power; the efficacy of our effort* or *freedom*. The Quran recognises the power of the individual to purify their inner being, or to debase and corrupt it.[91] The elements of our moral character that are not amenable to change are not objects of obligation or responsibility.

Being happy or sad, pessimistic or optimistic, by nature does not dictate morality any more than physical disabilities. Moreover, we must distinguish between the suggestions inspired by our inclinations, against which we can do nothing, and our will. The will does not operate in isolation of the rest of our being. It needs to look for motives which are found in reason and instinct. There is always a 'because' behind every voluntary action. Even when there is hesitation between two choices the ultimate decision is taken on the grounds that the choice was either equally as good as the other or better. *An indifferent will, is an imperfect will.*

In the ethical realm the will is always exclusive, it is both positive and negative: I want this not that. This supposes a motive, that is, self-interest or duty. The soul is made in such a way that it never makes any choice without being satisfied that there is some appropriate connection between the measure to take and the good to be attained. By definition, *will is the pursuit of finality.* The act of willing is not a natural continuation of previous acts as the Quran declares that this is not possible given human limits.[92]

The freedom which conditions responsibility must rule human nature rather than be ruled by it. Despite our feelings, temperaments, ideas and habits we are free to make decisions. It means we possess something higher than this collection. This does not make it independent of our unique makeup but underscores the flexibility of these elements within human nature. To will something is to order it. It is the beginning of a series. Before acquiescing to any design or motive, the will first imbues it with certain colours; it transforms it into a rational formula, by adding this protocol: 'I adopt this maxim as a rule for my behaviour'.

The decisive moment in the process of decision making requires a factor beyond those of tendencies, feelings and ideas. These have persuasive power, and may influence decisions but they are not the factors that actually bring one of several possibilities into existence. That factor is our total self: the end judge which determines the value of a particular aim, decisively endorsing a particular motive. This total self manages the interplay of our faculties in a way that enables us to orient our choice as we wish. In other words, we creatively adapt to either opposing aims. Everybody feels within themselves the power to stop a particular course of action. If we do not, it is because we choose not to. This is a natural freedom.

There is also a specifically moral power, a strict duty. The first power is that to choose between opposites. The second is the *good use* that we make of the first. We must effectively possess this power over the two opposites. Despite the pressure of internal and external nature in support of one choice, we can still choose freely without constraint or necessity but this is distinct from actually choosing what is good. When the self makes its choice on the side that meets the most resistance (assuming that this represents greater respect for the law), it calls upon reserves of potential energies in order to compensate for the deficit of the forces present. This effort will give greater credence to the chosen course.[93] The total self is the ultimate arbiter of our powers, not only approving them but more critically commanding them so that they are at our service. This is how morality occurs and how responsibility is engaged. It is not in the actual occurrence of the event, nor in the lack of strength of your senses, but in the contribution that you make to it, in the final colouration which you imprint upon it, in the seal of authority that you place on it.

Moral responsibility is asserted whenever an intentional decision takes place, whatever the seemingly irresistible compulsion of a physical, social or moral nature. The Quran asserts four essential elements in this regard:

1. The impossibility of foreseeing our future actions.[94]
2. The individual's power to improve or to degrade his inner being.[95]
3. The powerlessness of any suggestion to really influence our decisions, it is we who must accept or reject them.[96]
4. The severe condemnation of actions resulting from passion or blind imitation.[97]

Yet, exceptions to responsibility are to be found when tangible influences from the outside, like the threat of an aggressor or hunger, lead us to commit acts that would otherwise be reproachable. There is no blame in intentionally and voluntarily breaking the law but without willingly doing so, that is, without the express aim of breaking the law. Rather, the aim is some other object, for example, to save a life. In this regard the Quran states:

> *Whoever disbelieves in Allah after his belief – except for he who is coerced and whose heart is secure with faith – but he who invites disbelief into his breast, on them is the wrath of Allah... (Al-Nahl 16:106)*

> *...but whoever is compelled by hunger [to eat of that which is forbidden], not inclining willfully to sin, then surely Allah is Forgiving, Merciful. (Al-Ma'idah 5:3)*

The preservation of life is required by our instinct and commanded by moral law. Thus, yielding to vital necessity may mean relinquishing one's duty to perform another which conditions all other duties. Exceptions, however, are not valid for murder, theft or rape under compulsion from an outside force even at the cost of one's own life. This is because, although life conditions all other duties, it does not occupy the highest duty. Faithfulness to convictions is an even higher calling for humanity to guard its dignity. Moreover, it is possible that we exaggerate the risks of a situation, or that we repeat an action that was at first accepted due to serious threat but in which we found some pleasure or benefit. Erring on the side of endurance and self-sacrifice to avoid the implications of these prospects is recommended. It is clear that action, even under extreme pretexts, is too complex to garner acquittal but rather it is encompassed by forgiveness and clemency in the Quran.

The will in the Quran is presented as free and autonomous in its relationship with internal and external acts of nature. However, this does not mean that the Author of nature is irrelevant to our activity. God created all the energies in the universe, including our faculty of the will, according to a well-established plan; He knows in advance how each one of them is going to work and which events are going to be produced form the way they work, but it is not revealed whether or not God intervenes in the functioning of all these forces once they have been set in motion. Predestination means divine foresight. The Quran states that God has created everything.[98] It is also states:

> *Allah does not wrong anyone, by so much as the weight of an atom. (Al-Nisa 4:40)*

Surely Allah does not wrong people in any way; rather it is people who wrong themselves. (Yunus 10:44)

This means that God gave us the means that are necessary to undertake our duty. In other words, our will yields to the divine will, with respect to its efficacy and the achievement of results. Thus, to procreate is not to give life to the embryo[99] and to plant seeds it not to cause the seeds to grow.[100]

Our will depends on creation for its very existence and the way in which we exercise it is also dependent on divine authority of the Creator. If the will could free itself from this order, there would be multiple orders within the supreme order. The unity of the universe requires and proves the unity of its direction. Moral evil may go against His legislative will but not His creative will. Our acts are always in agreement with divine law. No supernatural act prevents them. In addition to this negative agreement, God has also surrounded our faculty of choice with a powerful complex apparatus from which all our decisions emanate: our intelligence, senses, tendencies, attractions, spiritual values as well as the inner light of conscience and the outer light of revealed and non-revealed teaching. Any decision, good or bad, is like a debiting transaction out of the vast account which God has put at our disposal in internal and external nature.

Justice demands that this human power be available to every person. However, it does not preclude that God has placed all people in equally favourable conditions for them to will what is good. Innate characteristics impact our decisions and judgments.[101] The Quran classifies people as rightly guided or misguided, both owing their respective states to God. In the Quran, God intervenes in positive and concrete ways when needed in order to remove certain people from evil temptations,[102] prevent them from indecency,[103] and strengthen their resolution.[104]

The invitation to peace is universal but guidance is reserved for whoever God desires.[105] Thus, noble souls acknowledge that any good they perform is due to God and they seek His continued support.[106] But this good is not granted with partiality or arbitrariness. Instead, it intervenes in favour of people who are worthy,[107] grateful,[108] pursuing and inviting it.[109] Those who reject faith are likewise abandoned since intervention cannot be futile.[110] In other words, those who are led astray have chosen corruption[111] while those He guides return to Him consistently.[112] Moreover, such divine interventions do not affect the moral action directly, overriding human will. Only supports are provided to ease our efforts so that our soul can soar but the final decision remains ours. The same is true of those who are left to wander in darkness.

The question of whether God stands away completely once He has placed these universal and personal resources at our disposal has not been answered conclusively in the Quran.[113] Engaging in such discussion is futile and can only result in conjecture. This is not an excuse to dismiss responsibility. In the end what is moral is the way we view our actions not the process of their production (the examination of our conscience when we are about to make a decision). When we act we do so of our own volition, not as instruments of God, since there is no way of knowing His divine will in advance. We accept the chosen action as our own. This is why the Quran proclaims our responsibility before God while it seemingly subordinates human to divine will.[114]

The Social Aspect of Responsibility

Responsibility toward God and ourselves must be *personal, voluntary and freely performed with full consciousness and awareness of the law*. But how does this apply our responsibility toward people?

In Islam limitation of criminal responsibility is to the normal adult person. Islam has stated: children are entirely free of responsibility until marriageable age, the insane until they recover their mind, and animals under all circumstances.[115] The culpability of children, the insane and even animals was not uncommon in the customs and cannons of societies around the world up until the 18th Century. Islam did not undergo the historical evolution that we have witnessed around the globe. This is the revolutionary character of Muslim law.

The Quran further protects individuals from corporal punishment in the case of involuntary manslaughter providing instead for compensation and expiation. Punitive responsibility is close to moral responsibility in Muslim law, though with some important distinctions. Morality is concerned with internal action. Punishment, in contrast, requires an external deed. Reprehensible intentions without actions do not entail legal responsibilities. Decisions made internally constitute moral deeds that may or may not then be outwardly expressed. This gives rise to new responsibilities or augments existing ones.

Retributive justice requires external evidence as to the action of the will. However, it can never be firmly established.[116] Because evil is decided by the rule of the will, as soon as one changes attitude toward the law they are forgiven. The Quran is full of hope for those who repent. Punishment can be averted except in cases of open rebellion.

> *Except for those who repent before you overtake them. So know that Allah is Forgiving Merciful. (Al-Ma'idah 5:34)*

Even when repentance is evident and sincere, it is not sufficient in the legal or social realms to warrant acquittal though it is in the moral realm. The resulting action has already produced negative implications for the victims and society. Thus, the person, property and dignity of others must be protected from loss, hurt and insecurity.

Unlike penal and moral responsibility which suppose that the intention goes against the law, civil responsibility is satisfied with the mere existence of the will, that is, the intention does not necessarily go against the law but an error or mistake has nevertheless been committed. The Quran sets out the principle for manslaughter.[117] In another sphere, it emphasises the responsibility of cattle owners who neglect to enclose and guard their herds that then cause damage to their neighbour's field.[118] This is reinforced by a prophetic narration in yet another sphere, outlining the civil responsibility of doctors before they are licensed.[119] Thus, people are responsible even when their action is not intended. Compensation in these cases tends to be financial.

This does not completely preclude moral responsibility as the mistake ultimately arises from some form of negligence or lack of competence. This is why the Quran also commands measures that support the purification of the soul even in exceptional circumstances. Thus, in the case of involuntary manslaughter, the Quran requires expiation in addition to financial compensation of the victim's family. A Muslim will have to liberate another individual from bondage or oppression and failing that he or she will have to fast for two consecutive months.[120]

These are preventative measures to guard against recidivism as well as to discipline the soul and help it heal.

Another distinction of civil responsibility is its collective element. Compensation to a victim's relatives is provided by the collective to which the perpetrator is affiliated, whether through a natural, conventional or professional relationship. If that is not sufficient to make one's share of the burden reasonable, then the state must intervene. A mistake is neither an intentional action nor is it a pure mistake. Thus, complete responsibility is not just but neither is no responsibility. The involvement of the community helps to attenuate this concern and keeps moral and social responsibility in conformity with each other.

It is not that the community carries any guilt with the individual who mistakenly carries out an action. But they are, as a group, responsible for their members well-being and as such cannot abandon those who inadvertently fall in difficulty. Each individual community member contributes in accordance with their ability,[121] which in turn contributes to social cohesion and solidarity. Moreover, the state is required to keep a fund for the relief of individual debt.[122]

Conclusion

The Quranic notion of responsibility is premised on personality. This means that it is individualistic, that is, not hereditary or collective. It is also premised on considerations of normal adult maturity, awareness and consciousness of obligations at the time of action, and freedom to act. Will and freedom are synonymous. No force, internal or external in nature, can influence our will. Such forces can deprive us of ultimately executing decisions but they cannot prevent inspiration of the will. Even as we consider external constraints, we ultimately choose in accordance to what we think is best and for this we are accountable.

CHAPTER 3

Sanction

Our relationship with the law is presented to us in the form of a back and forth movement, composed of three phases. Obligation is the starting point and sanction is the end point. The law starts by appealing to our good will, and obliges us to respond. As soon as we answer 'yes' or 'no', we bear our responsibility. In response to this answer, the law interprets our attitude and gives its sanction. In essence, sanction is the reaction of the law to our attitude. It is comprised of three domains: moral, legal and divine.

Moral Sanction

We speak of moral sanction because of the consequences that we benefit or suffer on account of the law's observance or negligence. Without sanction, moral law would be inefficient, random or irrational. A moral sanction consists of the satisfaction to have succeeded or the sorrow to have yielded unworthily when a duty is in question. This means that the law is meaningless for those who have lost their sense of good and evil. Every form of conduct, whether good or evil, gives rise to a corresponding inner state, which is both universal and necessary.

Remorse and satisfaction, however, are not sufficient rewards or penalties of moral law. These are reactions of our conscience to itself as opposed to a reaction of the law toward our behaviour. Through this process we become aware of our power to turn our ideas into deeds; to reconcile our reality with the sense of our ideal. We try to reach internal equilibrium. This is the definition of moral faith in Islam. Our inner reproach reflects the intensity and sincerity of the faith that we experience or the magnitude of our sins in conformance to the strength of our sense of obligation.

A violated law is not reinstated by a feeling of remorse but by the new attitude of the will or repentance. Remorse is the initial stage of healing but it may amount to nothing if we do not leverage the resulting discomfort to change our behaviour. Repentance is not a natural result of conflict but it is a sanction, which is properly moral and which involves effort. It is a new duty that the law imposes on us because of our failure to perform the first one.[123] Moreover, one cannot delay because every moment in the reprehensible act constitutes a new error.[124] One cannot continue to wrong oneself and offer repentance only at the end of one's life.[125] The forgiveness of a sin is only assured to those who repent immediately or in a short time.[126] This is not to deny that repentance is available throughout one's life, as the Prophet had stated, it is to emphasise that one can never know when that life will end.

The restitutive function of repentance in Islamic ethics demands an attitude that looks at the past, present and future and is manifested through actions, not only by adopting a new line of conduct, but also by the practical reconstruction of the edifice that has been affected. The Quran states that in addition to returning to God one has to mend one's ways by *doing good, doing it properly, and consistently.*[127] Repentance demands three actions:

1. To desist from the wrongdoing immediately;
2. To make amends for the past; and
3. To participate in a better future.

It is important to realise that correcting the past depends on the nature of the wrong that was committed. If it is a duty that can yet be fulfilled, then this must be completed.[128] If in contrast the wrong committed resulted in a hurt or damage then making amends required compensation. This does not change what has already transpired but served to diminish the effect of the act. The Quran states:

> *Good actions efface bad [ones]. (Hud 11:114)*

> *And others have recognised their sins, they mixed good works with other bad ones, maybe Allah will forgive them… Take alms from their wealth to purify and enrich them and pray for them, surely your prayers are a relief to them. (Al-Tawbah 9:102-3)*

Two types of error are distinguished by tradition including those which violate a personal duty considered as God's rights, and those which violate the rights of others considered human rights. The latter makes a further demand on the sinner in that he or she must obtain a clear and precise acquittal from the victim.[129] If that is not possible, the individual can expect to face his victim on the Day of Judgment. The Prophet had explained that this will consist in a transfer from the offender's good deeds to his victims' account. Any balance yet to be settled will then involve the transfer of the victim's bad deeds to the aggressor who will repay them for the victim in lieu of not having enough good deeds to give the victim.[130] Thus, all human error can be pardoned by God, except those committed against other people, since that must be subject to their agreement.[131]

Two more comments are in order regarding Quranic injunctions: (1) converts to Islam are exempt from all preparatory measures as coming into Islam removes all sins;[132] and (2) any relapse on the part of one who has repented does not diminish the initial act of repentance so long as it was performed with sincerity. The critical point is to renew one's efforts and not to lose heart and hope.[133] This discussion covers only restitutive sanction.

Retributive sanction demonstrates that doing good and abandoning evil have a real impact on our beings. These acts do not only impact our sensibilities but our higher faculties as well. Retributive moral sanction consists in merit or degradation; that is, in the gain or loss of value. The book of the truly good is in *'iliyun*; that of the dissolute is relegated to *sijin*.[134] The law seeks to put our entire being at its service.

The Quran asserts that the law is made for man and man is made for the law, meaning that man is made for himself.

> *And I have not created jinn and mankind except that they should worship Me. (Al-Dhariyat 51:56)*

> *Allah does not want to tax you, but He wants to purify you and to complete His blessings on you so that you*

may be thankful. (Al-Ma'idah 5:6)

The law is an end, but not the ultimate end. It is only a median term between man, such as he is, being born to morality or struggling for perfection, and man as he is meant to be, in possession of an integral virtue; between the ordinary man and the saint; between the soldier and the hero.

Truth and falsehood in the Quran are compared to two trees:

a good tree whose roots are firm and whose branches are in heaven. It yields constant fruit (Ibrahim 14:24)

A rotten tree, uprooted on the surface of the earth, with no power to endure (Ibrahim 14:26)

Acts of virtue and vice therefore have practical implications, good increases our value and raises our position, while vice has the opposite impact. Virtue has innumerable benefits. Properly performed, prayer has a dual moral function, namely, restraining obscenity and misconduct and extending spiritual communication with God.[135] Likewise, charity purifies the soul by turning it away from excessive attachment to wealth and brings relief.[136] Fasting has an eliminatory role: it keeps us from evil, protects us against the power of the senses; and thus, enables us to respect the law even more. It is a way of achieving piety.[137] Finally, the constant practice of virtuous actions makes a person sensible, courageous and generous.[138]

In contrast, vice leads to further evils. Drinks and games of chance, for example, consist of dual misdeeds: *they stir up enmity and hatred* between people and *prevent them from thinking of Allah.*[139] Lying is presented in the Quran as *the greatest of all depravities*, presenting it as the characteristic of an unfaithful soul, and therefore incompatible with (moral) faith.[140] Vice also affects our intellect, distorting our sense of truth,[141] whereas the balance of righteousness enables a person to discern the true and the false, good and evil.[142] All of our faculties receive their share of moral sanction. It is therefore our entire soul which is to be redeemed and perfected, or darkened and degraded.[143]

Legal Sanction

Legal sanction largely means punishment including penalties enforced by criminal courts. Here retributive sanction loses half of its meaning. Material rewards are not provided for normal duties. Instead, a person gains by benefiting in various other ways, for example, being protected by the law, participating in society, enjoying social esteem, holding various offices that demand high moral standards.

There are two forms of legal sanction commonly held in Islam – *hudud* which are strictly fixed maximum penalties and *ta'zirat* which are discretionary penalties. The first covers a limited range of criminal activity, treason, theft, drunkenness, indecent assault and false accusations of indecency. All the remaining belong to the latter.

The absolute character of the *hudud* is what distinguishes them from other sanctions. Once the crime has been brought to the attention of public and competent authorities it must be rectified in the public interest. Moreover, Islam emphasises equality before the law without exception.[144] Modern sensibilities that shun the severity and strictness of Islam's penal code diminish the importance and objectives of the law in achieving social order while directing sensitivities toward a higher moral order. Thus, values like faithfulness in marriage, security of person and property, reputation and dignity all take precedence over potential sympathy for criminals.[145] The offenders only have themselves to blame for subjecting themselves to such consequences.

One must also note that the exemplary nature of punishments ought to render them minimally applicable. The seriousness of the sanction makes the crime less attractive. The Quran ensures that the conditions for proof of guilt are extremely stringent and without compromise. This means that the maximum punishment cannot be applied should any of the criteria be missing or compromised. For instance, the number of witnesses in the case of adultery and the nature of the act they must have personally witnessed must be strictly satisfied for the application of the punishment. Because of this, not a single case of adultery was condemned in Islamic tradition based on testimony. Rather it was based on voluntarily confession. Even then, there are conditions that must be met by the confessor and the context. As a general rule, Islam insists on the innocence of the person and holds life including body, goods and dignity as strictly sacred.[146]

Moreover, Islamic law is adamant about the privacy of individuals. The Quran forbids spying on others,[147] thereby eliminating a great source of possible evidence for informers. Wrong done in private belongs to the judgement of God, not of people.[148] As compassionate human beings who are not without fault ourselves, we can make the choice to overlook and be discreet.[149] The sporadic wrongdoer deserves our confidence.[150]

A critical element in all this is that the perpetrator does not boast of his private exploits and sinful behaviour. The Prophet had warned of the unseemly tendency in some individuals to publicise what in the least should be kept private. By doing so an individual increases their immorality and exposes others to their exploits. Some, however, choose to come forward as part of their act of redemption.[151] It is therefore not necessarily the law, but each individual person who can be harsh or lenient toward themselves.

Except for a limited number of crimes, Islamic law does not specify correctional action. The role of justice is thus not only to establish facts but to prescribe appropriate penalties. This requires consideration of the seriousness of the betrayal of duty, the character of the accused, the circumstances of the offense, and the feelings of his victims (when it is a matter of an offense committed against someone else). Accordingly, the penalty varies from a simple, private reprimand to a more serious public reprisal.

Thus far we have established that moral sanction acts on the human soul aiming at the absolute, while legal sanction acts upon our external senses and aiming at the social order. Both are concerned with worldly reality, i.e., our present condition. The Quran, however, presents us with a third type of sanction, namely, divine sanction.

Quranic Exhortations and the Place of Divine Sanction

The Quran is very parsimonious when it comes to commands that are framed purely in terms of an authoritative voice. In fact, there are about ten passages of this nature.[152] They nevertheless include implicit motives. Although faith requires unconditional submission to divine commands,[153] however harsh they may seem,[154] it is at least equally true that underlying such commands is an advantage or benefit that may not always be explicitly discernable.[155] Divine command is in the least enveloped in truth and wisdom so that it gains the acceptance of our conscience.[156] Beyond this exception the Quran supports all commands in one of three ways: internal justifications, considerations of attitude, and considerations of consequences.

A. Internal Justification

Internal justification means that a moral value is inherent in a particular obligation. The value is positive when there is a command and negative when there is a prohibition and by association an act of disobedience. Internal justification is objective when it concerns issues of truth and falsehood, justice or injustice, or subjective when it concerns insight or blindness or purity or impurity of the heart.

Value is derivable from three possibilities: the particular nature of the object, the previous state of which it is the effect, or a subsequent state of which it is the cause. This means that when we judge the object we give it a certain value, either because of the values that it possesses in its own meaning, or because of those that it reflects in recalling its origin, or those which it produces and embodies. It is through a deep and extensive analysis of both sides of any action or rule that one may assess its value completely, sometimes by considering the thing in its actual state, in its determined agreement, sometimes by showing the course of its inception, sometimes by going to its immediate or distant effects. In all cases, as it is a matter of ethical judgement, the value referred to must possess the same quality as the object, and their relationship must appear to be a natural and not merely a conventional relationship brought about by legislation.

The texts to which we shall refer shortly have been selected in order to refer to this dual condition. They form considerably the largest, purest and most objective method of preaching in the Quran. We are urged to morality by and for morality. The fact that falsehood and evil pass away and lead to nothingness is not even mentioned; or that truth and good remain and bear everlasting benefits. Attention is drawn essentially or exclusively to their intrinsic characteristic as such.

In preaching its general doctrine, the Quran simultaneously reveals the truth about itself. As it proclaims, it is not a profit-making business; it is not an institution designed by its founder to make him rich.[157] It is not a discipline which rules by constraint, but a message to be transmitted, a teaching offered to a free conscience.[158] Neither is it the work of a poet,[159] or a diviner,[160] or a dreamer.[161] It does not arise from madness,[162] or from satanic inspiration,[163] or deceitful inventions,[164] nor the expression of any capricious desires.[165] It is the divine light,[166] which shows the right way[167] and puts you on the right, or the straight path.[168] It is the best discourse.[169] It is the established doctrine,[170] serious and decisive,[171] conforming to pure nature,[172] and to the middle path.[173] It continues and confirms the correct tradition.[174] It constitutes justice,[175] truth,[176] evidence,[177] science,[178] wisdom,[179] unshakeable steadfastness.[180] It provides healing to hearts,[181] ennobles the soul,[182] and life (in its most sublime meaning).[183] These are the characteristic features of the general doctrine.

If we now proceed from the whole to the particular, from the general doctrine to specific principles, we shall also find the main practical virtues, either required for their own sake (most often without any commentary), or established as objectives predicated on particular actions, or as sources of value for the human soul. The positive commandments that fulfill these conditions are to be found in the passages below, which prescribe or praise: the care taken to enquire into one's duties and teach others theirs;[184] moral effort;[185] conforming to good examples;[186] balanced actions, which hold the middle path;[187] righteousness;[188] striving to perform what is good or even best;[189] the most beautiful actions;[190] the best words;[191] sincerity;[192] chastity and decency;[193] the wise personal use of things honestly acquired; [194] courage, endurance and constancy; [195] gentleness and modesty; [196] circumspection in judgements; [197] doing good in general; [198] doing good to our parents in particular, [199] treating them with honour, obedience, tenderness and concern; [200] treating our spouses well;[201] kind conversation with them and mutual consultation; [202] supporting the needs of our families, in proportion to our resources; [203] paying compensation to wives in cases of divorce; [204] helping your near and distant relatives, [205] and neighbours, [206] travelers, [207] the needy in general[208] – help which is fittingly taken from excellent things that are properly obtained. [209] Supporting the poor and orphans in times of famine; [210] freeing captives; [211] uprightness; [212] generosity. [213] Equity, [214] as represented by the vertical balance of the scales, which tilt neither to the right nor to the left. [215]

Giving precise statement in all required testimonies, [216] whether it is against our relatives or ourselves; [217] returning what has been entrusted to us to its rightful owner; [218] being faithful to any engagement undertaken, word given, or oath sworn; [219] practicing hospitality and selflessness; [220] tolerance and generosity toward the ignorant; [221] returning good for evil;[222] inciting good and diverting evil[223] – all believers are united on this point.[224] Encouraging harmony[225] and charity;[226] the cooperation of all to help virtue and discipline prevail;[227] mutual exhortation and personal commitment to patience and mercy;[228] attachment to holy union;[229] consolidating all our sacred relationships;[230] affection for the spiritual community[231] and praying for it (showing community spirit); [232] the wisest and most honest ways of preaching the truth. [233] In brief, all ways of acting which are acknowledged and approved by reason and tradition.[234]

In the same category some examples of our duties toward God include to believe in God; [235] to obey Him;[236] to meditate on all His words and acts;[237] to remember Him;[238] to acknowledge His blessings;[239] to trust Him;[240] to make promises in accordance with His will;[241] to love Him;[242] to worship Him.[243] All these commands are justified by their own statement.

Below are the moral honours that are inherent in the action itself, which the Quran uses to motivate the will: the good, or the greatest good;[244] the most outstanding good;[245] a real good that goes against your immediate feelings;[246] more beautiful;[247] more just;[248] more precious;[249] the criterion of heedfulness;[250] the requirement of charity;[251] the requirement of heedfulness;[252] the requirement of gratitude;[253] the requirement of courage and magnanimity;[254] the requirement of selflessness towards the weak;[255] the requirement of consideration for the desolate, with whom we empathise, either by imagining ourselves in their place,[256] or by remembering our own past, when we were in pain, ignorant or lost,[257] or simply by being conscious of the condition of people, having need ourselves of divine clemency.[258] It is of a nature that will purify the heart or make it purer.[259] It is of a nature that will make the soul shine, enhance its power[260] to express thoughts more directly and to touch the heart more effectively;[261] it will maintain or reinforce the soul,[262] bring it peace,[263] remove doubts,[264] and keep one away from immorality,[265] bring it piety or nearer to piety,[266] prevent the committing of an involuntary injustice and the ensuing remorse;[267] reconnect the soul to God.[268] It is the quality that confers value to any command, however disproportionate to its quantity.[269]

It is notable that the Quran does not limit itself to considering the moral elements separately from our temperaments, conceptions, beliefs and ways of behaving. Because these elements are unified within us, the Quran sometimes explains and praises some through the others. Indeed, practical virtues derive part of their value from the fact that they reflect one's faith and prove its sincerity.[270] Faith, in turn, takes its value from being the privilege of humble and particularly sensitive hearts,[271] a particular state of the mind of which knowledgeable people have unique privilege,[272] a general Quranic teaching, which is manifest to people who are endowed with understanding, capacity to learn, reflect and deepen their knowledge.[273] To listen to its warning is therefore the first manifestation of life,[274] but to adhere to its doctrine is to exhibit clear thinking[275] and mature reasoning.[276] To practice it, as it was by the Prophet, is moral greatness.[277] Best of all, to practice it with others is to build a community into the best nation in the world.[278] These are the formulas of moral praise.

This way of teaching virtue through itself, without any other justification except that which comes from the moral concept and analysis of its own characteristic, is also found in the 'negative' duties, which forbid evil actions or condemn their disgraceful nature. The texts which formulate what is forbidden include: to commit suicide;[279] to commit indecent assault or any action leading to the crime;[280] to engage in prostitution or fornication,[281] or any other sort of immorality, openly or secret;[282] to lie;[283] to boast;[284] to follow uncontrolled desires;[285]

to imitate the unbelievers;[286] to covet other people's goods;[287] to hoard money and love riches excessively;[288] to strut arrogantly;[289] to dress indecently;[290] to make use of illicit gain or employ anything impure both physically and metaphorically;[291] to commit infanticide whether pressure is real or anticipated;[292] to show any disrespect to our parents in their old age;[293] to mistreat our spouses (through humiliation, extortion, deprivation or anything else);[294] to shed blood *which God has expressly consecrated, if it is not by right*;[295] to cause ruin or corruption on the earth;[296] to display aggression, even towards enemies;[297] to use or worse to take another person's property without their consent;[298] to touch the property of orphans, except in the most honest manner (in order to increase its value for them);[299] to reject orphans;[300] to do any violence to them;[301] to treat them disdainfully;[302] to neglect the poor;[303] to scold people asking for help;[304] to choose poor-quality objects as gifts;[305] to give presents out of self-interest;[306] to remind people of your generosity;[307] to be a false witness;[308] to commit any breach of trust;[309] to enter anyone's home without asking their permission and first greeting them;[310] to withdraw from any gathering without permission of the host;[311] to slander other people;[312] to spy on their secrets;[313] to slander and mock them;[314] to taunt them with derogatory nicknames;[315] to plot an injustice or act of aggression;[316] to break our sacred relations and create schisms;[317] to forget God;[318] to lack faith in Him;[319] to disobey Him;[320] to associate anything whatsoever with Him;[321] to abuse His name.[322] All of these prohibitions are already justified by their own statement.

Here, however, is how the Quran gives them express justification. In opposition to the positive values included within virtue, we find that here the anti-value contained within vice is emphasised. Any behaviour which is contrary to the established rule, as well as any lack of faith in superior truths is condemned, not because they lead the offenders to perdition, but because they imply, simultaneously or individually, the following errors: going astray;[323] carelessness;[324] walking in darkness;[325] deviation from the right path;[326] the wrong path;[327] reversal of values;[328] walking unsteadily;[329] falling;[330] following desires blindly;[331] worshiping passions;[332] miserable exchange;[333] choice of an accursed companion;[334] walking behind the enemy or alliance with him;[335] using bad names;[336] imitating the unjust;[337] resembling something ignoble;[338] resembling something loathsome or repulsive;[339] blindness;[340] deafness;[341] ignorance;[342] lack or wrong use of intelligence;[343] limited knowledge;[344] superficial understanding;[345] refutation of what is not known in depth;[346] disputation without knowledge or guiding light;[347] upholding of a position which has neither certainty,[348] proof,[349] nor experience.[350]

Bad judgement;[351] destroyed argument;[352] no sound basis;[353] fragility;[354] extreme fragility;[355] imitating ignorant and erroneous forebears;[356] adhering to simple conjectures;[357] falsehood;[358] unreality;[359] only names;[360] deceitful inventions;[361] Satan's inventions;[362] aberration;[363] careless attitude, way of those without sense;[364] exaggeration, going beyond limits;[365] evil action;[366] lewd action;[367] shameful unworthy action;[368] hateful action (which makes us despicable to ourselves);[369] corrupt, irregular, unruly behaviour;[370] unjust behaviour;[371] sinning against oneself;[372] a great blunder;[373] a crime, great sin;[374] sin of the heart;[375] self-betrayal;[376] impurity of the heart;[377] despicable moral outrage;[378] failing;[379] skepticism;[380] lack of commitment;[381] acting according to self-interest;[382] hardness or heart;[383] unjustified pride;[384] pretending to be interested in and enthusiastic about everything;[385] words contradicted by actions;[386] attachment to this world;[387] being distant from God.[388]

The most natural conclusion to draw from this accumulation of errors is to agree with the Quran that they produce, not only the darkening or eclipse of the soul;[389] not only sickness or infirmity of the heart,[390] but the death of the spirit.[391] Those who have stubbornly decided to be unfaithful are viewed as the worst of all, the lowest of creatures on earth.[392] This suffices for the list of blameworthy actions.

B. Considerations of Attitude

This aspect does not constitute sanction but rather a transitory state, an intermediary zone that leads to sanction. The Quran clarifies that we are never alone. Above the guardian angels appointed for each one of us[393] is God for whom:

> *Equal among you is he who keeps his words secret and he who articulates them orally, and he who hides by night and goes forth by day (Al-Ra'd 13:10)*

> *... and you do not do any work except with Us as witnesses over you (Yunus 10:61)*

God is nearer to man than his jugular vein and hears what his own self entreats.[394] Thus, God knows everything we do and all that is in our hearts.

Through these statements the Quran seeks to remind us of reward and punishment, irrespective of the knowledge of others and their common judgement of our behaviour. From a simple, beneficial piece of advice to the stating of a sanction, it has diverse warnings of varying gravity. Thus, within this intermediary zone we can speak of attitudes that represent primary stages of an integrated and continuous process. Each has a mode of exhortation.

(1) A clearly welcoming attitude, favourable toward order and discipline, although to varying degrees. Here God's presence is perceived and welcomed within a loving framework. A believer will find in this idea that which really sustains his efforts, nourishes his energy, raises up his soul, multiplies the demands on himself, not only to keep to his chosen direction, but also to keep watch over the quality of his actions and the purity of his intentions when they do not always bring what is new and better. There is no doubt that the remembrance of God at the moment of the action is constant source of energy for the faithful affecting their will and strengthening the desire to perfect their behaviour and to perfect themselves. This is the guaranteed way of attaining constancy and continual progress. The Prophet made it the very definition of perfection. "What is it to do good?', he was asked; he replied: 'To do good is to obey God with the same presence of mind as if you were seeing Him; and if you do not see Him, surely He sees you.'[395] The feeling called forth by this mode of exhortation is akin to that of being comforted, of a supportive power.

(2) An attitude of being generally well-disposed towards the law, but not excluding the possibility of sin. Here commands are given in abstract form. It does not directly stimulate the effort towards good, nor does it crush evil tendencies. It remains vague, being in the middle; it is both at the same time. One no longer reads: 'God sees the good you do,' nor yet:

'Be careful not to do evil', but: 'such is your duty; God will see what you do.'[396] The decision can go either way. This is the duality reflected in a believer.

(3) The attitude is still one of complacence in principle, but since the existence of some particular circumstances may introduce some change, the tone becomes more serious. Abstract formulation continues, however, denunciation – due to a potentially greater possibility to violate the rule is evident.[397] This exhortation largely leads to feelings of modesty. We do not want to commit acts which would embarrass us in front of God.[398] If we falter, it is because of temporary lapse caused by the pressures of life.[399] So the first stage is love, the second is self-control, and the third is modesty.

(4) Finally, the open rebellion of the unfaithful. Here a clear position is determined which defies the law. Crimes are presented that are then followed by avoidable outcomes.[400] This represents a distant warning addressed to the reasonable being buried within them. Perhaps they may reflect. Nothing is said of the consequences of actions at this point.

C. Consideration of Consequence

Natural consequences: only a few passages in the Quran refer to 'natural sanctions' or the outcomes that result from the routine order of things. Four passages are associated with commands motivated by the good of the individual:

> *And do not give the foolish any of their property over which Allah has made you custodian, but provide for them and clothe them out of it (Al-Nisa 4:5)*

Do not ask about matters which, if they were known to you, would harm you (Al-Ma'idah 5:101)

... and the women of the believers that they should dress modestly so that they will be known and not harmed (Al- Ahzab 33:59)

Lastly, the condemnation of greed and extravagance is justified in one place by the fact that they lead respectively to *blame* and *destitution*.[401] Then there are commands justified by the moral good.

And not equal are good deeds and bad deeds, repel with what is better and he with whom you have enmity will be as if he was a dear friend. (Fussilat 41:34)

Satan wants to sow enmity and hatred between you by means of wine and games of chance... (Al-Ma'idah 5:91)

The prohibition of murder must refer only to the guilty for:

and there is a life for you in qisas (Al-Baqarah 2:179)

In case of conflict, the duty to keep on guard and not put down one's arms, even during prayer, is imposed as a precautionary measure against a surprise attack.[402] Fighting is only for the *cause of God*. It is only to attain this ultimate aim that the texts mark out several intermediary stages to:

a) Stop the violence of the unbelievers, breaking their aggressive power.[403]
b) Prevent corruption and disorder from spreading throughout the earth.[404]
c) Safeguard religious institutions against destruction.[405]
d) Punish the aggressors and relieve the hearts of the faithful.[406]

In these passages we are dealing with practical common sense, the instinct for self-preservation, a legitimate sense of self-respect and a praiseworthy concern to promote mutual friendship among people. In other words, self-interest is the aim of moral law. This suggests that morality is no longer to be an aim unto itself. Yet, in times of conflict between self-interest and duty, we yield to the sovereign order of duty. In all other matters we cannot ignore our self-interest.

In other words, we cannot with any measure of credibility, isolate our sense of duty from instinct, intelligence, faith, reason and self-interest when they all direct us to the same decision. Once there is an evident motivation, an objective, it cannot be ignored. The will cannot shield itself from all that we consider valuable. Indeed, it is our direction toward these inseparable elements that endears duty to our hearts.

This does not diminish the value of duty in and of itself. Rather, it is a educational technique that eases individuals, who start at different degrees of acceptance, into this process. The Islamic approach justifies and offers something in exchange for what it proposes to take by showing that the path of duty is also that of intelligence and refined taste, of redemption and exaltation. Over time we come to appreciate the value and pleasure of a moral life, thereby distinguishing it from external motives and the deceptions of natural events. In short, the Quran demonstrates through the examples just noted that the natural order is involved in our moral concerns, interacting with them, and producing results which deeply affect us.

Non-natural consequences (or *divine retribution*): not all virtues and vices find their reward through the natural order of things. In other words, natural sanction is not universal. Beyond the inherent satisfaction of moral behavior, there is no logical link between virtue and happiness. If we considered virtue, however, as something we are obliged to undertake as an expression of gratitude, we recognise that the good for which we give thanks is already present.

Generally, we do not expect society to reward us for the normal performance of our duties. We owe it more than it owes us. In turn, we owe much more to God, the Creator. He who gave use our existence, our faculties, our energies, our possibilities and gifts, material and spiritual. In light of this, our good behaviour ought to be perceived as a repayment of a debt, an expression of gratitude for the infinite blessings which the Creator has bestowed on us, even without having asked for them.

The link between our actions and virtue is clarified in the Quran. The certainty of accountability is presented irrespective of how we perceived or felt regarding our actions when we undertook them.

> *Does the human being think that he will be left aimlessly? (Al-Qiyamah 75:36)*

Without this link, happiness and virtue remain separate in our minds. It is our will, fortified by our hearts and minds, that intervenes to harmonise future happiness and virtue. The immortality of the self and the existence of God are starting points in the Islamic ethics and are the foundation of the system of sanctions. God is Creator, Legislator and Judge. The individual who is fully committed to his actions will eventually reap full consequences of his or her actions. And just as the law of duty is established by God through voluntary action so is the general principle of retribution.[407]

The link between good and happiness, evil and punishment and the separation of the just and unjust is presented in the Quran as fact:

> *Nay, do those who do evil deeds think that We will make them like those who believe and do good, so that their lives and deaths will be equal?... (Al-Jathiyah 45:21)*

> *Or shall We render those who believe and do good as the corrupters in the earth? Or shall We render the heedful as the transgressors? (Sa'ad 38:28)*

> *Shall we then render those who submit as the criminals? What is with you? How do you judge? (Al-Qalam 68:35-6)*

Retribution cannot be rationally determined. It can never be due to our actions in and of themselves but rather is the subject of a promise, a contract between God and the individual.[408] How can the acts of a finite life lead to infinite rewards? The grant of Paradise is due to divine generosity.[409] But is nevertheless based on divine promise due to our actions.[410]

Divine Sanction

The nature and modalities of divine sanction: The Quran makes the promise of happiness in this world and the next. Divine retribution takes place at two levels for the just as well as the guilty.[411]

A. Divine retribution in the present represents a very limited portion of divine sanction, which is more fully expressed in the moral, spiritual and intellectual order.

The Quran expresses this kind of reward as follows:
a) *The Material Aspect*: virtue will have one part of its reward in this life and the other greater part in the life to come. Only one passage promises material benefit in this life.

Whoever is heedful of Allah, He will give him an outlet and provide for him from where he had not contemplated (Al-Talaq 65:2-3)

The material aspect is more explicitly articulated in these passages:

And whoever is heedful of Allah – He will make ease of his affairs for him. (Al-Talaq 65:4)

The notion of goods provided to good people is of a general nature.[412] Happiness is presented as follows:

And ask your Lord for forgiveness and then turn to Him, He will please you with a goodly pleasure until a determined time, and will give any who bestowed favours their due. (Hud 11:3)

The vast majority of Quranic teachings related to the implications of morality for material aspects come through the transmission of ancient stories or those contemporary to the Revelation. Thus, we read that people who become ungrateful toward God and act accordingly are made to taste deprivation.[413] Yet others are chastised for their exaggerated confidence in their future thereby neglecting the power of God,[414] or for their oppressive behaviour toward others toward whom they bear a duty.[415] In other words, human destruction is due to what humans themselves earn.

And if the people of the towns had believed and been heedful of Allah, We would have opened up for them blessings from the sky and earth... (A'raf 7:96)

And if they had upheld the Torah and the Gospel and that which was brought down to them from their Lord, they would have consumed from above themselves and below their own feet… (Al-Ma'idah 5:66)

And if only they were to stay the Path, We would have quenched them with abundant water. (Al-Jinn 72:16)

When corruption becomes rampant, God reacts in the Quran by eliminating entire populations.[416] This sets the example for those who are to follow who are neither better nor more powerful than their predecessors,[417] rather it is quite the contrary.[418] Evil doers can be overcome in land and sea,[419] in sleep or wakefulness,[420] on their travels[421] by a number of ways.[422] Moreover, it can be sudden or gradual.[423] The main idea is to convey to the rich and powerful that they are vulnerable in the face of God's power.

b) *The Civic* Element: represents the collective dimension of retribution. There are numerous direct and explicit promises to believers who suffer on account of their faith and service to God. If people are patient and steadfast, they will not be harmed by the scheming of their enemies.[424] God is with those who heed Him.[425] He grants them victory,[426] and helps and elevates them.[427] For those who strive for just causes and support its defenders, the Quran states:

Allah has promised those among you who believe and work righteous deeds that He will surely make them successors in the land, as He succeeded those before them, and He will establish for them their religion that He approved for them; and He will exchange their fear for security… (Al-Nur 24:55)

The earth shall be inherited by my righteous servants. (Al-Anbiya 21:105)

The enemies, in contrast, are destined to defeat and regret.[428] They are promised inferiority.[429] Covered with humiliation,[430] their power will be destroyed.[431] Public morality is paramount in governance. It is therefore conceivable that a secular empire can last and prosper in union and justice much longer than an empire of so-called believers who are in fact dishonest, disorderly and wicked. In this regard, the Quran states:

And if you turn back, He will exchange in your place an-

other people, and they will not be of your example (Muhammad 47:38)

c) *The Intellectual and Moral Elements*: to continue to do good one requires support and guidance. How do we choose one path as opposed to another? To those who strive towards Him, God will show the paths along which He prompts them.[432] He will guide their hearts;[433] He leads them out of the darkness into the light;[434] He will guide them on the straight path;[435] for those who observe truth and righteousness in their words, He will rectify the sins of their actions;[436] to those who piously observe His commands, He will give the power to discern true and false, good and bad;[437] He will grant them a guiding light.[438] As for those who have faith and do good deeds, He will forgive their sins and given them peace of mind.[439] Those who welcome guidance, He will increase their light, guide their steps and increase their heedfulness.[440] He causes tranquility to descend upon their unwavering hearts in order to consolidate their faith.[441]

As for the unbelievers, the unjust, the proud, the aggressors, the ungrateful, the sceptics, the tyrants, the liars, those who commit perjury, the corrupt, the slaves of passion, all those who have specifically chosen to be the enemies of the faith, not only does God not direct them,[442] but He: maintains and increases their misguidance;[443] has hardened their hearts;[444] has sealed up their hearts, their ears and their eyes;[445] made them deaf and blind;[446] has increased their sickness;[447] prolongs their error and their blindness;[448] has made them hypocrites;[449] made them forget themselves, by forgetting God;[450] has abandoned them to Satan;[451] who guides them towards darkness.[452]

These moral reactions are not just meted for the unjust but also for those who forget that their light and inspiration are a gift from God. If they lose their humility and forget this fact, grace may be withdrawn as a consequence.[453]

d) *The Spiritual Aspect*: here our actions determine our relationship with God, which has affective value and is primordial in its existence and its importance. The main question here is whether or not we are worthy of His love. In the Quran we read:

Allah loves those who do good (Al-Baqarah 2:195; Al-Imran 3:134, Al-Ma'idah 148; 5:93)

Those who are just (Al-Ma'idah 5:42)

Those who are patient (Al-Imran 3:146)

Those who are pious (Al-Imran 3:31; Al-Tawbah9:108)

Those who put their trust in Him (Al-Imran 3:159)

Who fight in His way in rows like a well assembled structure (Al-Saff 61:4)

He accepts their pious deeds (Al-Hajj 22:37)

He remembers those who remember Him.[454]

All kind words and good works are elevated to Him (Fatir 35:10)

Those who, when afflicted with tragedy, say 'To Allah we belong and to Him we shall return.' They are those on whom descend blessings from their Lord and mercy, and they are the ones that receive guidance (Al-Baqarah2:156-7)

Allah was pleased with the believers when they pledged their allegiance to you [for His cause] (Al-Fath 48:18)

and with those who follow His will;[455] who profess their gratitude to Him;[456] who do not ally themselves with His enemies, even if they are close relatives.[457] It is also He who has inscribed faith in their hearts and:

Reinforced them with a Spirit from Him (Al-Mujadilah 58:22)

He is *with* those who keep themselves from wrong doing and practice charity.[458] He is their patron.[459] Finally, the more people are heedful of God, the greater their dignity in the sight of God.[460]

Statements of the opposite kind represent a break in our relationship with God. Rejecting faith and its rules earn His displeasure. For example:

The evil of these actions is hateful in the sight of your Lord (Al-Isra 17:38)

Corruption and corruptors[461]

Aggressors [those who attack first or go beyond reasonable force] (Al-Baqarah 2:90; Al-Ma'idah Al-A'raf 5:87; 7:55)

Those who are unjust (Al-Imran 3:57, 140; Al-Shura 42:40)

The wasteful (Al-An'am 6:141; Al-A'raf 7:31)

The treacherous (Al-Anfal 8:58)

The arrogant (Al-Nahl 16:23)

The unfaithful (Al-Imran 3:32; Al-Rum 30:45)

The proud, vainglorious (Al-Nisa 4:36; Al-Hadid 57:23)

The ungrateful and sinners (Al-Baqarah 2:276)

The liars and the wrongdoers (Al-Nisa 4: 107)

Allah does not accept ingratitude (Al-Zumar 39:7)

The negligent (Al-Tawbah 9:56)

Allah does not like the broadcast of vile words, except in the case of those who have suffered an injustice (Al-Nisa 4:147)

God dislikes words that are betrayed by actions.[462] Through their unfaithfulness, the impious draw upon themselves the abomination of God,[463] as well as through their unfounded disputes against the revelations of God.[464] The wrath and curse of the Most High is not reserved just for

the obstinate disputers:[465] renegades;[466] unbelievers in general;[467] murderers;[468] those who break their oaths;[469] calumniators;[470] deserters.[471] It is also directed at the so-called believer who, leaving his community, seeks the guardianship of evil-doers, without being forced by necessity to do so thereby cutting himself off from God:
He has no relation with Allah (Al-Imran 3:28)

Insufficiency of the immediate sanction: divine sanctions in this life are no more universal[472] or complete than the natural or human ones.[473] In other words, it is what we do in our lives that results in various sanctions. Sovereign justice must necessarily go beyond this. Good people suffer the consequences of their sins in this life,[474] just as mean people reap the benefits of what good they do. In the last judgement, however, happiness and misery will not be mixed. Instead, each group will reap the rewards of its worldly state, i.e., the good will achieve blessedness[475] and the bad anguish.[476] This, however, is not the entire story. The good or bad that befalls us in this life cannot only be viewed as recompense for our deeds but may also perceived as incentives or challenges to our efforts.[477]

In order to satisfy the manner of these three points a purely retributive sanction is elaborated in the Quran. This is the result of our effort.

B. Divine Sanction in the World to Come

The Quran deals with divine sanction in various ways.

a) Passages that only state the eternal abode of the just or the guilty as Paradise or Hell respectively.[478]

b) Passages that express the destiny of individuals in an indeterminate way are also numerous. For the just is: good news;[479] hope;[480] a fine promise;[481] triumph;[482] immense goodness with God;[483] fruitful efforts[484] acknowledgement;[485] recognition;[486] success,[487] a good end;[488] profitability.[489] People who have done good will be greeted by their own good deeds,[490] which will be even more enriched,[491] and which will be returned to them in full,[492] and multiplied,[493] according to the best of their actions,[494] with a extra granted by the grace of God. [495] Their reward is assured,[496] a magnificent, splendid reward; [497] better,[498] generous,[499] forever;[500] an honourable and pleasant stay;[501] a fulfilling life;[502] a blissful life.[503]

Just as frequent but less differentiated is the warning to the evildoers. These will be paid back in kind.[504] For the infidels, the unjust, the hypocrites, the proud, the criminals, all transgressors will be reserved unhappiness, an evil stay, and a severe punishment, a painful, ignominious everlasting chastisement.[505]

c) Passages concerning the nature of Paradise and Hell, and the transitory period between this life and the next.

A foretaste: When the just are called to surrender their souls, they receive the good news awaiting them:

Peace be upon you! Enter the garden for what you did. (Al-Nahl 16:32)

The martyrs especially will be:

> *Delighting in the favour that Allah has bestowed on them, rejoicing for the sake of those they left behind who have not yet joined them (Al-Imran 3:170)*

As for the damned, they will experience a harsh reality:

> *And if only you could see the unjust in the throes of death when the angels are stretching out their hands, saying, 'Expel your own souls! Today you will be recompensed with the punishment of humiliation.' (Al-An'am 6:93)*

> *And if only you could see when the angels take back those who were unbelievers at their death, beating their faces and their back: taste the torment of the fire (Al-Anfal 8:50; 47:27)*

Not much is mentioned in the Quran regarding the interval between death and resurrection. Here we only have two references to the people of Noah and those of Pharaoh respectively: *after they were drowned they were put in the fire* (71:25); and, *they are exposed to the Fire, morning and night* (40:46). This is reinforced by certain Prophetic narrations regarding the fate of unbelievers during this interval.[506] In contrast to passages on transition and interval, the Quran offers detailed accounts of the physical and moral elements of Paradise and Hell.

Paradise: Spiritual joys: First, the spiritual aspect of celestial bliss is defined in negative terms by the following promises: peace and safety;[507] absence of sorrow;[508] exemption from shame;[509] forgiveness of faults and effacement of sins;[510] mercy (inasmuch as it consists in sparing God's loved ones from evils).[511]

Positive spiritual joy. The blessed have a life of: kinship and reciprocal love (free of any malice);[512] contemplation of the divine beauty;[513] contentment and joy;[514] honour and glory.[515] Their happiness will cause their faces to shine;[516] they feel superior to the opponents who mocked them.[517] As they journey towards Paradise, their light will go before them and to their right.[518] They will enter into the society of the great and virtuous,[519] with their families and friends.[520] On arrival, they will be greeted by the angels with the words:

> *This is your Day, the one that you were promised (Al-Anbiya 21:103)*[521]

Once they are settled, angels will *enter in from every gate* bringing them congratulations and wishing them peace. [522] Welcomed by the All-Merciful, they will be given 'good tidings'. [523] He will say to them 'Greetings!' [524] He will bring them near; [525] He will raise them to high degrees;[526] they will have fine seats next to the Almighty Sovereign;[527] they will obtain his pleasure.[528] The satisfaction is reciprocal;[529] they will be pleased on two accounts: content with themselves (because of their past striving),[530] and pleased with their fate. So they will ceaselessly praise God for having guided their steps and keeping His promises to them.[531] Futile, frivolous talk, sin and accusation of sin will be banned from this dwelling of happiness.[532] One only hears the exchange of mutual greetings,[533] and praises for the Almighty.[534]

Paradise: Material happiness: It is here that the Quran promises the righteous the absence of death,[535] protection against all evils,[536] and the removal from the realms of torment.[537] It also promises rest;[538] in a word, salvation.[539] In Quranic language, the synonym for Paradise is the *abode of Peace.*[540]

Paradise is described as *an immense garden, so immense that it is as wide as the Heavens and the Earth.*[541] Here one enjoys the freedom to walk and rest whenever one wishes.[542] A garden where there is always shade[543] and the climate is always temperate, without excessive heat from the sun or severe cold.[544] It is a happy and refreshing place,[545] with rivers flowing through it,[546] rivers of water that is forever pure, rivers of milk whose taste does not alter, rivers of delicious wine [that does not intoxicate], and rivers of purified honey[547] and fountains of water[548] variously flavoured, with which to mix the exquisite wine.[549] In these blessed places various fruits grow[550] in abundance and offer themselves on branches within reach[551] which never break,[552] nor are forbidden.[553]

Then imagine that, on this green carpet threaded with sliver are buildings,[554] with many stories[555] constructed beside the rivers, or beneath which rivers flow,[556] luxuriously furnished, with thrones and high seats,[557] seats which are studded with gold and precious stones,[558] cushions, rugs and table sets,[559] decorated with materials lined with silk.[560]

Then imagine these splendid palaces teeming with a kind of high courtly life on a grand scale, during a brilliant reception. A united gathering: men, women, children, grandparents, friends, all in their best finery and decorated with jewels,[561] clad in silks,[562] of restful hues,[563] leaning comfortably in their seats,[564] turning affectionately to face one another,[565] conversing pleasurably and recalling past memories.[566] Absorbed in their bliss,[567] they only have to ask for what they wish.[568] To serve them are young men endowed with eternal youth, like hidden pearls,[569] bearing in their hands golden cups and dishes,[570] jugs and glasses[571] and other vessels of silver.[572]

They will have provisions,[573] morning and night.[574] They hasten to offer them what they wish: drinks,[575] dishes,[576] sweetmeats.[577] In short, anything they desire will be granted to those who served God faithfully.[578] All their wishes will be granted,[579] and more than that.[580]

Nevertheless, the highest values are given to spiritual things and the moral value always surpasses the physical. Thus we are told to envision:

> *Purified spouses (Al-Baqarah 2:225; Al-Imran 3:15; Al-Nisa 4:57)*
>
> *Virtuous first, then beautiful (Al-Rahman 55:70)*
>
> *With modest gazes first, then with large eyes (Al-Saffat 37:48)*
>
> *With modest gazes, then, of the same age (Sad 38:52)*

Virtue is always prioritised in Islam, both in this world and the next.

Hell: Negative and moral punishments: the negative moral punishment for the damned consists of the following: their deeds are worth nothing.[581] Deception in their expectations of the idols they had associated with God.[582] They despair of God's mercy,[583] of His absolution,[584] of His vision,[585] His gaze and His justification;[586] their deprivation of the light (which they vainly try to find close to the believers),[587] of sight, hearing, speech (at the time of resurrection),[588] of all their hopes;[589] their despair of eternal life[590] in which they will have no part,[591] where they will be neglected,[592] abandoned,[593] rejected,[594] without any help or ally.[595] The gates of Heaven will not be opened for them.[596] Their pleading will not be heard.[597] In brief, they will see their failure,[598] and loss.[599]

Hell: Positive moral punishments: At the resurrection, the evildoers will appear before God with bowed heads.[600] Their faces blackened,[601] severe and despondent,[602] covered with dust and grime.[603] On that day, they will wish that a great rift would separate them and their evil actions,[604] but the Book is there, wherein everyone's actions are recorded, down to the smallest detail.[605] Moreover, their own bodies and their sense organs will testify against them.[606] Their crimes will be loaded on their backs,[607] and they will carry about the goods which they hoarded,[608] reviled;[609] blamed;[610] hated.[611] Covered with shame and humiliation,[612] they will file past their Lord, while spectators look at them and point at them with contempt.[613] Taking hold of their account, they will wish not to have known it and that death would truly be the end for them.[614] Seeing at last their merciless retribution approach,[615] feeling all the links with their leaders and associates break,[616] unable to wind back the course of time and to return to earth,[617] they will only be able to bite their nails and sigh with regret.[618]

Hell: Physical punishments: the physical sufferings endured by the unjust after the final judgement can be first presented in a negative form, which consists in the deprivation of essential needs. Hungry and thirsty, they do not find anything to alleviate their hunger and their thirst.[619] However, the Quranic passages which define their punishments positively far outnumber these.

Diametrically opposed to the celestial mansion of the elect, the abode of the damned is a prison[620] with several entrances, each one designed for a particular category;[621] a prison whose guards are robust, harsh angels;[622] an abysmal prison divided into several vaults going deeper and deeper underground.[623] It is fully closed.[624] It is a ditch filled with fire,[625] fervent fire,[626] which can be heard from far away roaring with rage,[627] like an erupting volcano,[628] throwing sparks as large as castles.[629]

The damned are tied up with their necks, hands and feet bound.[630] Attached to long chains,[631] they are dragged face down,[632] thrown face first into the fire,[633] restricted to the narrowest space,[634] enduring excruciating torture.[635] They experience the pain of incineration,[636] as they become fuel for the fire.[637] Paralysed with anguish and sorrow, every time they try to escape their agonising pain they are pushed back into the middle of the fire with iron clubs.[638] They are surrounded with torment.[639] Their faces are battered by the flame,[640] which will tear off their skin,[641] burn their flesh,[642] and reach their hearts.[643]

The piles of gold amassed by the greedy will be melted down in the fire, then spread over their faces, flanks and backs.[644] There will be cries of sorrow and pleas for mercy.[645] They will sigh and moan.[646] As soon as their skin is burnt off, another one will be put on them, so that they can taste the torment once more, and forever.[647] Being cremated is not the only torture: they will alternately be plunged into boiling water.[648] It will be poured onto their heads to make their skin and entrails melt;[649] when drinking it their faces are roasted and their intestines torn.[650] They will have another beverage so foul that they will hardly be able to swallow it.[651] There will also be the fruit of *Zaqqum*, which will boil in their stomach like molten lead,[652] and other foods that choke and other painful tortures,[653] such as burning wind,[654] the artificial shadow of smoke,[655] or extreme cold alternating with extreme heat, according to some commentators on the world *ghassaq*.[656] Suffering and affliction without respite.[657]

Though the punishment is physical the intent is moral suffering and humiliation.[658] and there will be no one there to help them. All that is left are disputes,[659] hatred,[660] and mutual cursing.[661]

Conclusion

Quranic ethics take both the individual and collective conscience into account. It does not draw its authority exclusively or even primarily on a transcendent will that asserts itself though reward and punishment. Instead, the human soul is the holder of natural moral law, breathed into it at creation. The Prophet advised everyone to consult their own soul to learn the duties that they are to undertake.

Human reason is endued with its own specific domain of appreciation and legislation. Our reason, however, may become obscured by life's circumstances and by our desires. When we struggle between feelings and reason, the later becomes the final judge. Without doubt, the reasonable will is the most excellent part of our being; it is specifically ours, whereas the rest of us is similar to other inferior natures; it is the only faculty that is able to concentrate us within ourselves, whereas the senses and instincts scatter us outside. Thus, God conferred upon the will the right of leadership and principal role of organiser.

However, in addition to the law primordially imprinted in

our nature there is the positive and explicit law that comes from God. The latter serving to reinforce what is inherently existent in every human being, albeit in its purest form. From this point of view, the framework which is set up by this positive law to allow the free and legitimate exercise of individual conscience will not only draw a line between what is licit and illicit, but also between what is truly reasonable and what is not. Islamic legality does not supplant morality but rather acknowledges and refers to it continuously. When formulating its commands, the Quran appeals to their conformity to reason, wisdom, truth, justice, righteousness, among other values which form the very structure of the moral conscience. The Quran emphasises the consequences of virtue for our souls and how our behaviour influences our hearts and minds, as well as the significance of remorse and repentance.

Human beings are also social beings. The role of the Islamic community in establishing moral authority stems from *ijma* or unanimous decision of the competent legislative body, declarations from executive power that serve to preserve order and welfare as well as administrative details legitimately prescribed because it draws power from moral law. Thus, considerations for society mean that those who commit wrong are punished when apprehended even if they repent. The idea is to support communal life – despite the fact that the conditions of both morality and faith have been satisfied in the sincere act of repentance. Reparations to society go beyond divine satisfaction.

Behind the individual and communal conscience is the order of universal nature with its law of causality. Good leads to good and evil to evil. Consequences are only there to encourage duty, and must not deviate from it. Quranic ethics comprises these considerations (moral requirement, essential social necessity, and sound practical sense) and surpasses them and successfully perfects them through a much higher principle: faith in a sovereign legislator, whose sublime authority is indispensable to the approval and sanctification of any decision taken elsewhere.

Quranic commands are thus supported by: (1) the sole legislative authority of God to whom obedience is owed;[662] (2) the sense of His beautiful omnipresence encouraging us to do good to the best of our abilities; and (3) the consideration of sanctions established by God. People will receive the moral, physical and spiritual rewards for their actions in this world and the next. The Quranic notion of sanction seeks the human soul in all its powers and its depths. It means to appeal to all human beings of all classes and levels of intelligence. The command of duty must find its justification in truth in whatever form it may take, it must be able to prevail upon the soul, from whichever angle it sees it. The supreme authority of Quranic duty is established through the majesty of the divine order, its conformity to wisdom, its identification with good in itself, the satisfaction that it gives to the most noble and sensitive feelings, the moral values that its application is destined to realise, and its glorious aims for this life and the next.

CHAPTER 4

Intention & Inclinations

Intention is defined as the movement by which the will *tends* towards something, either in order to *achieve* it or to *obtain* it. The immediate object of the acting will is the action that it is determined to accomplish, but this undertaking can only be fully voluntary if a person sees some good at the heart or the periphery of the action, which justifies it in their own eyes and which is its reason for being. It is the mediate object, the ultimate end towards which the intelligent and conscious effort inclines and which it intends to reach.

This distant object is called an end or aim, insofar as it is the reality to be pursued and attained; but inasmuch as it is a concept or an idea which instigates and prepares the voluntary activity it is called a *motive* or an *inclination*, two terms which are generally considered synonymous even when they have enough differences to give our representations different roles in the preparation of an action. As a motive the idea of a good outcome plays an essentially intellectual role; it serves to justify the intended action, to make it reasonable and to show that it is legitimate, but once this intellectual stage has been passed, the idea of the aim becomes a motivating force which pushes our activity forward; from the point of view of this influence on the will it is called an inclination.

Our essential starting point in this chapter is the clear distinction between two types of objective of the will: the *what* and the *why*. We take it for granted that in a normal carefully thought-out decision, the will necessarily observes two things: one which bears upon the action and the other upon its conclusion. Thus, we can say that, intention is that which is related to action and inclination is that which bears upon the conclusion.

Intention

An intention (*niyya*) is a firm decision, *'azm, qasd*. It is the attitude of an awakened mind that is aware of what it is doing or is about to do. Intention must have the following three elements:

(1) To understand what one is doing;
(2) To want to do it; and
(3) To want it precisely because it is commanded or prescribed.

It is therefore the consciousness that we have of our voluntary action, either when it is about to be executed, or is in the progress of being so, while knowing that, through it, we are proceeding with an obligatory task.

Thus defined, the notion presents a number of problems that need to be resolved. What would happen if the intention were made completely or partially in error? To what extent can the intention change the nature of the action? When a moral deed is performed does primacy belong to the action or the intention? How far can the intention alone fulfil the role of a perfect duty?

A. Intention as a Condition of Validity

Islamic law ignores actions where either or both knowledge and will are missing. What cannot be imputed to us cannot be characterised as good or bad. The same goes for conscious but involuntary action.

Legal and moral principles part when an act is voluntary, conscious but unintentional. Thus, the act may fulfill the material criteria of the law but not its spirit. Actions are only ours to the extent that we intend them. Thus, if someone performs an act on our behalf or forces us to perform a duty, as in the community or state or other responsible authority as part of their obligation to establish justice, this diminishes nothing of the claim against ourselves. The former undertakes the fulfillment of the act as part of another duty. So long as we do not participate willingly and with full awareness of responsibility, our duty remains unfulfilled. Thus, what satisfies social obligation does not do the same for moral obligation.

The Quran requires a moral consciousness in the most elevated sense of the term: consent of the heart, spontaneity of action, delight and eagerness with which one performs one's duty. This is why acts that are performed without sincerity are not accepted.[663] Indeed, those who profess an insincere faith are not counted among the believers.[664] The condition of morality and faith is that one accepts the law and submits entirely without reservations.[665] The Prophet had stated *innama al-a'mal bi'l-niyyat*, meaning that actions are judged according to their intentions or more precisely actions exist (morally) through their intentions. Morality and intention are inseparable. Moral validity can only be granted to an objective deed when the notion of duty is present in the conscience. Intention is a condition of moral validity for an action.

B. The Intention and Nature of Moral Action

This section considers the question of whether intention is able to bring fundamental change to the very nature of an action; whether, an evil deed made with a good intention acquires moral value and therefore becomes a virtuous deed and vice versa.

For now, let us accept that the value of the intention derives solely from the way in which we judge that intention, according to whether it agrees or disagrees with the law. It is understood that our moral judgements do not necessarily coincide with the reality of things, and it is quite possible for the will to deviate when it pursues something that might conform with or contradict with duty, but which does not do so in reality.

In fact, it is absurd to accept that good intention measured as conformance to the law alone constitutes a moral good. If it is material conformity to the law that matters, then evil intentions are just as acceptable so long as the substance of an action is beyond censure in the eyes of the law. Rather, one must accept that the conscience is empowered to change the nature of action. In other words, our internal views influence our external actions.

What if an action conforms to the law but the intention is not good? Whoever undertakes an action which is blameworthy in their own eyes, however lawful it is itself, commits a crime with regard to the moral law through their intention, despite its material conformity. What if intention conforms to the law but the act is not good? Evil actions can never be made good by the will. In fact, our thinking that it can constitutes another mistake: ignorance of the law and ignorance of what we do not know. The Prophet said, 'whoever commits an act that deviates from this command of ours, that act is rejected.'[666] Good behaviour requires good action and good intentions, neither is expendable.

The comprehensive instruction concerning duty is found in the hadith:

> 'God does not look at your outward appearance or your riches; He watches your heart and your actions.'[667]

Also,

> 'God does not accept a word which is not translated into action; and He accepts neither action nor word, if it is not spring from good intention.'[668]

The implicit implication in this discussion is that in order for a rule to be followed freely, it must be known. In short, no word or action is valid independent of its intention, intention is not valid unless it conforms to a duty, and knowledge is necessary in order for a rule to be freely followed.

This is a tall order but the Quran does not insist on our infallibility. Quranic ethics accepts that we fall into error and demands that we consistently seek to learn objective law and be guided by it, correcting ourselves as we proceed through life. We must never assume that this knowledge is complete but rather expend of ourselves to reach it. It is this effort that is our saving grace out of God's mercy.

Moral good is neither an internal state nor an external expression – it is both at the same time. The external expression may be beneficial for society but it's not so for us personally (except to gain materially). If the will is there but for whatever reason the action is impossible or incomplete, value is determined accordingly. But if the will is not present or corrupt, good acts have no value and may even be criminal.

C. The Prevalence of the Intention Over the Action

The prevalence of the intention over the action involves the analysis of the relationship between the decision making faculty and the power of execution in both the internal and external aspects of the latter. The Quran emphasises that the action of the heart and expressions of the body go together.[669] Whereas one never sees it praise a good deed which does not spring from the depths of the soul, quite frequently it mentions the action of the heart alone, either as a value in itself,[670] or as the most essential condition for eternal salvation.[671]

Tawqa of Allah, piety or being heedful of God, is an inner disposition mentioned more than 220 times in the Quran. By this term the Quran means an obedient and reverent attitude toward the divine order, which must be understood in its widest sense,[672] or in the particular sense of a prohibitive commandment, as opposed to the meaning of *birr*.[673] Both imply physical and moral conformity, but the Prophet stressed the inner aspect as the essence of virtue. 'This is where virtue is found,' he said pointing to his heart and repeating the gesture three times.[674] Although one cannot persuasively argue that internal acts provide people with the rights that they are due, the role of the definitive result in the fulfillment of a duty is put in perspective. Since the final result does not depend solely on our moral effort or on our physical activity, but needs a multitude of natural, or even supernatural conditions to work together, we find that our duty is considerably limited: it is restricted to using, but not to bringing to fruition, the means at our disposal. Because the moral aspect guides the physical

– good or bad – it is given primacy over it – even though it is further from the final result chronologically. It is a relation of causality rather than temporality.

The Prophet told us: 'It is through the health of the heart that the body is healthy, physically as well as morally.'[675] Internal action is a necessary condition of the objective good as well as the cause through the mediation of manifested action. Moral law is not only for establishing justice but to raise us above social matters and other creation in this worldly life. Physical action is thus of two-fold importance – it is beneficial externally and also internally augmenting our natural dispositions and making them deeply rooted. Thus charity strengthens the soul,[676] purifies people and increases our value.[677] This can be said of all good acts, keeping in mind that the physical remains a form of fortification of the will rather than its equal.

Intention has a privileged position in relation to external action but what about internal action? Thus, the need that we feel to improve our character may be determined either by a kind of natural vocation, or by a taste for perfection, or by a simple desire to use our creative powers, or to attain for ourselves an infallible conformity in our external behaviour, in order to ensure that we do not falter in public. The intention that we give to this process gives value to our inner effort. It is like the spirit of the spirit.

D. Can Intention be Enough by Itself?

Intention is always valuable, but the nearer it comes to action, the more it is enriched with values and it only attains its full value in the accomplished action. Divine justice weighs every degree of effort[678] with the minutest accuracy to the weight of an atom.[679] In a sacred, *qudsi*, hadith a good deed which has not been performed is counted as one, whereas one that has been performed is counted for ten good deeds.[680] The effort employed and sacrifices made are taken account of. Those who contribute with goods and their person are not equal to those believers who do not strive as such.[681] Thus, while intention is good and necessary , well-intentioned action is better and constitutes the complete moral deed.

Inclinations to Act

To sum up, the awareness of what we are doing and why we are doing it is the prime element in morality. The deviation of intention either condemns the act or is just enough to merit forgiveness. Out of the two constitutive elements of the moral deed, intention has primacy over action. Intention, thus, is a valuable moral good and is sufficient for itself but not for the complete moral deed. The conclusive aspect of the will, in contrast, is related to why we perform our duties in the first place.

It is not enough to note that the Arabic term *islam*, means both *inqiyad*, which is submission to the divine will, and *ikhlas*, which is the exclusion of any other rule over the human will. The Quranic emphasis on acting with pure intentions cannot be overstated. Therefore, it is critical to understand what purity of intentions means as well as the forces that can destroy it, e.g., mixed motives.

A. The Role and Nature of the Mediate Intention

The deepest intention is a criterion of value – a final condition of merit or blame. The continuation of the hadith 'actions are only judged according to their intention'[682] is 'and for each individual will be attributed only what he had intended.'[683] To further clarify, the Prophet continued, 'he who migrates for

God and His Messenger, then his migration is for God and His Messenger; whereas he who migrates for a worldly gain or to marry a woman, so his migration is for what he migrated for.'[684] It is clear that the role of the principle of moral judgment is only assigned to a genuine moral intention issuing from the depths of our soul, not from a superficial idea obtained through the artifice of words internally spoken, or outwardly expressed.

> *Truly, God knowledgeable of what is in the breasts (Al-Ma'idah 5:7)*

> *And whether you keep your speech secret or broadcast it, He is knowledgeable of what is the breasts...He is the Subtle, the Knower (Al-Mulk 67:13-14)*

Occasionally a believer is unable to discern his or her true motive. Instead of despair, the individual turns to faith, to God. On the one hand, the thought of the gentleness of divine law, which commands us not to go beyond our nature, is counterbalanced in our conscience by the idea of divine knowledge, which sees the depth of our hearts, knows the limits of our power and can judge whether or not we did our best to rectify our inner behaviour. On the other hand, the thought of this divine knowledge, which fills us with a moral anxiety and a more exacting attitude toward ourselves, is moderated by that of a mercy which is always present to welcome those who repent of their forgetfulness and try to repair their mistake, and to support them and provide them with increasing strength.

There are different categories of motives with their respective rules in Islamic ethics. In order to judge whether an intention is good, bad or tolerated, we must consider: the type of action we think is required to achieve a particular aim and the role which a particular motive is called to play within the force that motivates us (not all motivations have an equal influence).

B. The Good Intention

The believer obeys duty as something that corresponds to a fundamental reality emanating from God who endowed us with this reason, wherein He deposited primal truths, moral truth occupying the first rank. The Quran stresses that all rational beings were created to *turn toward their Creator in an act of love and obedience*. Our submission to God must be complete, unreserved and pure.[685]

By purity, the Quran means that our actions are not to be influenced by our desires.[686] Our will must also be free of external impurities, ethics cannot depend on momentary considerations including prestige, power,[687] rewards or recognition.[688] In light of this, the Prophet was commanded not to give so that he may have more.[689] The motive to do good can only be the desire to purify oneself, seeking only the approval of God.[690] To drive this point to its fullest expression, the Quran tells us that it is God that receives alms not the poor.[691] The Prophet reinforced this by stating that the one who gives to the poor 'places his alms in the palm of God's hand.'[692]

The definition of a good intention, then, is a movement by which the obedient will turns away from any object of desire, or constraint, whether it be internal or external, in order to turn to the direction from which it received the command. This is what we must respect when we act.[693]

This does not exclude a renunciation of the world and its pleasures but rather tempers them with the necessity of heedfulness toward God or *taqwa.*

> *O children of Adam, take your beautifications to the masjid. And eat and drink but do not waste, for Allah does not love the wasteful. Say: Who has forbidden the beautifications that Allah has brought out for his servants and the good blessings? (Al-A'raf 7:31-2)*

The development and advancement of life is inherent in the facilitation that forms a clear dimension of our existence. Enabling us to put to use those aspects of creation that we require.[694] But life remains temporary[695] and all of this is a means to an end.[696]

When we pursue worldly gains, six scenarios for the will are possible including:

(1) A love of wealth without limits leading one to the worship of blind desire;[697]
(2) A conformance to the law due to constraints but bemoaning of such restrictions;[698]
(3) Conformance to the law, not out of conscience but out of habit and preference;
(4) Conscious recognition that something is not prohibited so incline toward satisfaction of natural needs (self-interest rules not the law since the latter allows a number of alternatives). These options are thus morally worthless, though the vast majority of people operate in this zone.
(5) Actively attempting to give moral meaning to the acts that one performs. By giving valid reasons to the aims of what otherwise are mundane activities we infuse them with moral value. Thus, I exercise because the strength I

gain allows me to meet my obligations with greater energy. I work for something other than the pleasure of possession, e.g., to support those in need. What is perceived as self-interest emerges as morally valuable even necessary. (6) Finally, devotion of oneself to cultivating the heart and mind, only intermittently accepting material items for survival and giving up what one does not require[699] even if we have a right to it.

That said, it is also necessary for some believers to accumulate wealth with the intention of supporting those who do not have a capacity to do so. Thus, it is the moral intention that determines the superiority of the last two scenarios. Both perform the permissible and seek the moral good as its driving force and foundation. But even if we determine that it is the law that motivates us, we have yet to determine in what way it does so. The possibilities here include: out of a love/heedfulness for God, fear of punishment, hope for reward, concern for outcomes (good aims of the law), obedience to formal order.

The first of these possibilities is uniquely worthy of moral value. Here the intention is limited to the action and not in anticipation of any result. The purest intention is to be a subject of the divine, not a claimant against God. By leaving the results to God we put our hearts to rest and focus more satisfactorily on the present action. The benefits that complete impartiality can bring to the soul include simplicity of the objective, concentration of effort and inner peace.[700] Moreover, actions are better performed when we are not hurried for results. Moreover, disappointment will not result from unexpected results nor ecstasy from achievements since we have become detached from consequences. Nonetheless, these other considerations are not considered immoral.

Indeed, to take interest in the results of one's efforts is an important motivating force. The key is to remain balanced. It is to consider consequences to the extent that such consideration informs our proper duty or what, when and where it can be applied so as to achieve desired aims. For example, if an insurrection against a tyrant has no power to re-establish just order and only serves to harm innocent people and to make the despot more powerful than he was before, one must opt for the lesser evil. *Thus, there are conditions for any particular legislation. By increasing the awareness of our duty, consideration of results clarifies the status of an action by presenting the objectives which ought to shape our obedience.*

The *ends* that we consider may be objective or subjective. An objective end is independent of the actor even if he or she may derive some benefit concurrent with the performance of the act. A subjective end is an effect that the actor considers purely in relation to themself. The supreme principle of morality is found in the former, i.e., *objectivism of intention.* A good will does not ask for reward for its efforts. The Quran expresses this ideal from two different perspectives. The first involves the intention which stops at the abstract duty. The duty is undertaken in order to obey God because He is the Master, commanding obedience irrespective of justifications.

The second instance exhorts believers to penetrate the deep meaning of the command, and seek to align our own aim with that of the Legislator; we are concerned with establishing order, justice and truth; in a word, we aim to actualise the good which we know or presume to be the aim of the law. Thus, God commands believers to fight enemies in order to obey God but also to protect the weak and oppressed,[701] and to put an end to their suffering that prevents them from practicing their faith.[702] The Prophet referred to this as: 'Those whose aim is to make God's will prevail.'[703] Which one of these takes precedence depends on many factors as they do not contradict each other. An intention which aims for the deepest meaning of the command does not take away anything of the beauty of faith, but adds something to it, to build upon it and make it resilient. In fact, the two are indispensable to each other. The concern to perform the moral good which is revealed in explicit rules is never separate in the conscience of the believer from an instinctual feeling of unconditional adherence to all the rules without which the term 'believer' is not applicable.[704] Thus, for a religious ethics, both points of view act together and imply each other. Whether one stops at form or seeks to understand substance, one attempts to identify with the object of the law. We draw near through love and gratitude or keep a distance out of respect for the law.

Does all of this mean that subjective aims are blameworthy? By placing innocence between merit and blame, legitimate between praiseworthy and punishable, and tolerance between obligation and proscription, one removes the challenge posed by the pursuit of subjective ends. Thus, a person who guards his or her duties but also acts legitimately to provide for needs is safe according to prophetic tradition.[705]

C. Innocent Intention

An innocent intention arises when we act legitimately to avoid an evil end, while not claiming impartial devotion. These acts are legal, and do not warrant praise or blame, reward or punishment. In other words, they are neutral in the moral sense. These actions can be elevated from their safe status to praiseworthy and rewardable.

For this to happen, two conditions must be met: the end must be authorised by the law and known to be such by the subject. Any inclination must be subordinated to the rule which conditions the movement of the will. In employing exceptions to the rule under dire circumstances one must be sure that he is acting out of necessity and not inclination.[706] The rule comes first.

In order to determine whether we place our inclinations or self-interest above our duty we simply have to consider what we do in prohibited cases. If every time we are faced with a prohibition we breakdown and do what is best for us, then it is likely that we continue to do so when the law conforms to what we want. In other words, even in cases where there is harmony, we are likely continuing to behave out of a self-interest and not deference to the law. The Quran addresses this unstable character that relies primarily on self-interest.

The second condition to transition beyond a morally neutral act, is that the action which is taken must be of the kind that can morally serve as a means to reach that end. Here the idea of finality expresses itself in full complexity as within the same action one must be able to detect the objectives of the Legislator and those of the subject – both principal and secondary. While our principal aim is to fulfill a sacred duty without demanding any return from people or God – reaping the rewards of our actions – secondary aims - is premised on a promise not a right. Any reward is out of God's mercy and justice, as opposed to a right based on our performance. The reality is that fear and hope motivate us to turn to God, and the Quran tells us to resort to patience and prayer[707] at all times but especially in times of need. Indeed, this is the tradition of our Prophet.[708] Fear and hope, reward and punishment, cannot, however, be the justification for the performance of our duty. This would confuse two types of finality: the existential end (outcome) and the moral end (the aim) as well as overlook a critical factor required for eternal bliss, namely, a sound and pure heart.[709]

We must perform our duties for God after which, not in order that, we will find happiness. That said, happiness to the believer is a subordinate consideration to pleasing God. The Prophet had prayed:

> 'Lord, I complain to Your Majesty of my weakness, the small means that I have, and the negligible regard people have for me... If You are not displeased with me, everything else is unimportant. Even so, the salvation that comes from your Mercy will be sweeter to me."[710]

Two conditions are required for eternal bliss: purity of the heart and constant faith. But neither the promise of eternal bliss, nor severe punishment is sufficient for a believer to consistently respect these two conditions. This is why the Quran states that believers are simultaneously influenced by both fear and hope.[711] Between these two elements the believer is resigned to perform their duty, whatever may transpire. This results in *haya'* or a sense of modesty that guards us against shame in front of God. Indeed, sometimes satisfying a permissible good may give rise to a moral good. For example, in a Prophetic tradition we are told that we can earn a living for self-interest, or we can do so believing that our contributions make this a better world.[712] We can perceive of worldly comforts as blessings and mercy from God and through our acceptance we conform to His will[713] through which we show gratitude. 'God loves us to enjoy His generosity, just as He loves us to obey His formal commands.'[714] Indeed, to reject such mercy expresses the opposite attitude, namely, ingratitude. Finally, although the Quran disparages excessive play and distractions, the Prophet indicated that certain forms of leisure have value and were important for relaxation as well as the development of other skills and advantages.

The bottom line, however, is that such permissible actions, even when they are praiseworthy can only be subsidiary considerations in our quest to fulfill our principal duty to please God. This is the unifying principle of morality.

D. Evil Intentions

While there are innumerable paths of immorality, the Quran and hadith emphasise the following categories: intention to do harm; intention to avoid one's duty; intention to make an illicit profit; and the intention to please others (ostentation).

1. Intention to Do Harm

The best law in the world would be useless without the good will of the people to which it applies or who are to apply it. The worst attitude toward any law is to feign a pious appearance, carefully respecting it to the letter, while working to divert it from its aim, making it unjust and hateful instead of charitable and kind. In Quranic expression making a mockery of Allah's words.[715]

Thus, a man who refuses to divorce his wife merely to cause her grief is highly culpable and repudiated by the Quran even though he appears to follow the word of the text.[716] The same goes for those who devise legal wills to deprive their legal heirs under the pretense of helping other beneficiaries.[717]

2. The Intention to Avoid One's Duties

This is achieved by concealing the conditions of application or by instigating an event that is likely to change the legal meaning of the circumstances. The idea is not to hurt others but to avoid one's duties, though of course the former may result.

One's selfishness can be limited to isolating oneself from critical situations or social relations, while more extreme forms involve employing all possible means to gain self-serving gains. An example is to temporarily lend out one's money at the time of alms (zakat) giving to avoid or minimise the obligation. Or to conceal one's wealth and possessions to avoid giving the needy.[718]

3. The Intention to Gain Illicit Profit

One form is to disguise the true nature of an exchange by, for example, not disclosing the real properties of merchandise. The Quran demands the consent of all parties to an exchange[719] which implies that all elements of a transaction are explicitly set out. Fairness toward everyone and in everything is how the Prophet defined faith.[720]

Also troublesome are those who follow the word but attempt to find loopholes and tricks to gratify their needs. If God forbids something He also forbids any money to be derived from it.[721] The Quran categorically forbids usury, not only in its modern, restricted sense (fixing interest above a certain rate), but in the older broader sense of the term: any profit, material or otherwise, that one draws from those to whom one makes a loan. Lending is not trading; it is helping. Any tricks to disguise this are forbidden.

4. The Intention to Please People

This ill intention involves doing one's duty toward God and men in order to show off. Here an external source of motivation is sought to encourage one to act including approval, admiration, praise, etc. Of course taking care of oneself in public more greatly than in private is acceptable and required.[722] The trouble arises when such behaviour is intended for ostentation. It is important to distinguish between ostentation (*riya'*) and hypocrisy (*nifaq*), the latter is much more complex and involves the attempt to appear as something that one is not.

The refinement of virtue is so intense in the Quran, that we are not permitted to seek the attention of others as such. It renders our deeds worthless and worse condems our souls.[723] In a hadith, the Prophet stated that among the first to go to Hell are: (1) a man of knowledge who studies by night and day so that people will say what a great scholar he is; (2) a rich man who gives alms so that people say that he is generous; (3) a soldier who sacrifices his life with the ambition of being brave.[724] To want the praise of people is compared to idolatry by the Prophet as 'the most subtle form association.'[725]

E. Purity of Intention and Mixed Inclinations

The Quran requires us to have pure hearts focused on God as the sole object of its actions.

> *Whoever desires the meeting with his Lord must work righteousness and not associate with His worship anything (Al-Kahf 18:110)*

This is further explained by the Prophet when a Bedouin asked him the following: 'Messenger of God, man fights out of courage, or patriotism, or for fame, or ostentation. Which of these is in the way of God?' The Prophet replied: 'The one who fights with the aim of making God's word triumphant and exalted is the one who alone fights in the way of God.'[726] This hadith is very strict in purity of intention as it does not permit a single deviation from inclination to God's word. In a hadith *qudsi*, God states: I am the richest of the rich and will not have any associate. If anybody performs an action which associates Me with anything else, I abandon him entirely.'[727]

All motives added to the will diminish our moral standing and deprive our acts of God's approval. However, our inability to isolate our inclinations is not considered immoral and hence punishable. Instead, the ideal of purity is something to which we aspire. Regarding mixed inclinations, the Quran only ever says that it does not merit being called in the way of God; that it 'does not please God'; that it 'is of no worth to Him'; that 'God can ignore it'; and many phrases of similar import, which do not grant such acts a positive value, without necessarily establishing culpability. To feel good after the fact, or to take satisfaction in a job well done is not the same as to incorporate an inclination in the commission of the act. Here the decision to act has already been made, i.e., it is not contingent on external factors.

For those who mix a good action with a bad one, the Quran states, that they may still hope for God's forgiveness.[728] Although these represent two actions, not one with several motivations, the analogy is that acceptable motives similarly leave room for clemency. Nothing will be neglected in the final judgment and not the least bit of good will be overlooked. The key is to recognise our consistency. Would we offer the same aid to a stranger as we would to a friend? God always has to be at the forefront, that is, our primary motive.

Conclusion

Islamic ethics is not reduced to its physical expression. The regard for duty necessarily means situating an action in its relationship to the law. Duty must return to the realm of the conscience and be part of its objective. Otherwise it only has a material definition, remaining outside morality. Our intentions may be reason to excuse or condemn us. The preliminary condition of a moral deed is the presence of a will which proceeds to the action in its conformity with the rule and only as such. Both the moral choice of the immediate object (the action) and the distant objective (the end) must be morally good.

The Quran uses persuasion to win over our minds. The authority of Quranic duty is determined by:

(1) The majesty of the divine order;

(2) Its conformity to wisdom;

(3) The identity of its object with good in itself;

(4) The satisfaction it provides to the noblest and most refined feelings;

(5) The moral values which its application is destined to bring the soul; and

(6) The glorious outcome in this world and the next. The only valid aim for a believer is God. Our activities must be inspired, guided and directed by God's command.

CHAPTER 5

Effort

The second element in the actualisation of virtue is action. This unique part is both defensive and offensive. Whether it is a moral decision to be taken or performed, or the intimate trait of a character to be improved, or even an intention purified, the only help available to reach these goals are our moral and physical powers which are able to take us there.

It would have been both fruitless and unreasonable to exercise effort in trying to acquire virtue if the human soul had a complete and accomplished nature, or if, defective as it is, it was incapable of evolving. A moral being is created both imperfect and perfectible. We are neither complete nor immune to evolution. We are granted faculties that enable us to develop our reason and physical knowledge.[729] The soul is inspired at its inception with what will debase it and what will reinforce its piety.[730] Through the action of our will we can elevate or debase ourselves.[731] Thus, the moral necessity to act and bear responsibility.[732]

To exert effort is not merely to act. Rather it is to struggle with strength and perseverance. The Quran states that this is the condition of human nature.[733] On every page it extends this appeal to a sustained, ongoing struggle, either to perform good and resist passion, or to endure evils and master one's anger, or to put our religious duties into practice. We must obey God with all our strength.[734] This is what the Quran calls the *overcoming of the obstacle.*[735] This effort is the definition of sincere faith.

> *The believers are only those who believe in Allah and His Messenger and do not doubt, and strive with their wealth and their persons in the way of Allah, such are the truthful (Al-Hujarat 49:15)*

Effort and Spontaneity

Effort only has value when it is a means of producing something morally good. Virtue is neither the fruit of pure nature, nor is it completely acquired. A good person struggles against evil, while a wicked person has a seed of good that he or she can use to overcome their vice and bad habits. Whether innate or acquired everyone is different in the degree of what they possess. The Quran distinguishes between two types of effort.

A. Eliminatory Effort

This is the effort we exert to resist bad inclinations which tempt us to do evil. For those who accomplish this feat the Quran states:

> *So when the great calamity comes; the day on which humans will recollect for what they strove; and Hell shall be made manifest for those who will see; then as*

for him who was inordinate; and preferred the life of the world; the blazing fire will be his refuge; and as for him who feared the station of his Lord and denied the being uninhibited desire; then Paradise will be his refuge (Al-Naziat 79:34-41)

The month of Ramadan (annual fast) is one way to discipline ourselves by breaking the hold of our senses. God assists those who exert effort in His way.[736] In a hadith *qudsi*, He states:

'My true servant never ceases to approach me through supererogatory actions until I love him. As soon as I love him, I become the ears through which he hears and the eyes through which he sees.'[737]

The will is equipped in a way as to help it reject evil whether a person is one of faith or not (albeit to varying degrees). The Quran states:

...the self indeed commands to evil except such as my Lord bestows mercy (Yusuf 12:53)

The Prophet had warned that 'everyone is shadowed by a diabolic companion.' 'Even you?' someone asked. 'Even me', he replied, 'but my Lord has helped me conquer him and he has submitted.'[738] All devoted believers are subject to this favour.

Surely, he [Satan] has no authority over those who believe and in their Lord place their trust (Al-Nahl 16:99)

> *Surely, as for my servants, you will not have any authority over them (Al-Isra 17:65)*

Islamic sanctity is not indifferent to human nature, but consists rather in an heightened preference for spiritual values. The Quran does not say of the believers that they love God alone, but rather above all else.[739] Resorting to patience and prayer to ward off evil is indeed difficult. The Quran states:

And surely it is very hard, except for the humble (Al-Baqarah 2:45)

We must develop our abilities to lessen the effort that it takes to achieve virtue. We do this so that our actions express a form of spontaneity, that is, spring consistently from a deep rooted and stable source. Thus, extreme effort is only a passing phase that is eventually assuaged with our greater capacity to spontaneously choose the good. Instead, we come to approach our duties with energy and joy.

Thus, it is a victory of effort. This, however, does not imply our omnipotence or complete power. As the Quran confirms:

> *And as for those who strive hard for Us, We will guide them to Our Paths (Al-Ankabut 29:69)*

> *And as for those who settle on piety, We increase them in piety and give them their reinforcement (Muhammad 47:17)*

> *Surely as for those who believe and work righteousness, their Lord will guide them by their faith (Yunus 10:9)*

It is evident that our initiation of the struggle and demonstration of sincerity, is only one dimension of the process toward goodness. In the final analysis it is the grace of God that grants us the fruits of our efforts.

Even then our effort to walk the right path is due to the grace of God. Thus, we read:

> *Therefore whomsoever Allah desires to guide, He makes his breast welcoming to Islam. And when He desires to misguide someone, He constricts his breast, narrowed, as if he were rising into [outer] space (Al-An'am 6:125)*

> *Allah has written faith upon their hearts [true believers] and reinforced them with a spirit from Him (Al-Mujadilah 58:22)*

> *It is He who sent down serenity into the hearts of the believers (Al-Fath 48:4)*

> *Allah has endeared faith to you and beautified it in your hearts, and has made disbelief and lewdness and disobedience hateful to you (Al-Hujarat 49:7)*

This certainly does not preclude that the believer already demonstrates a favourable attitude.

> *He knew what was in their hearts and sent tranquility upon them (Al-Fath 48:18)*

> *It is He who sends down tranquility into the hearts of*

the believers, that they may add faith to their faith (Al-Fath 48:4)

Our status increases to the extent that the struggle is diminished. Value increases as the necessity of our effort decreases. But our efforts do not end there. After our struggle in the darkness, there is the struggle in the light. As soon as we are no longer preoccupied with fighting our *demons*, we are exhorted to an effort that is *productive* and *constructive*. Morality is not only or primarily about restraining evil, but about doing good.

The Prophet said, 'all muslims must practice charitable works.' He was then asked, 'what if they cannot?' to which he replied, 'let them work… for their own benefit and also in order to do acts of generosity.' Again, he was asked, 'what if they cannot?' to which he replied, 'Let them come to the aid of anyone in urgent need.' 'What if they do not?' 'Let them exhort people to right.' 'What if they do not?' 'Let them refrain from evil; for it will be counted for them as an act of charity.'[740]

After eliminatory effort then comes creative effort.

B. Creative Effort

Creative effort exhibits three degrees of intensity or quality. The first step in this process is to act, voluntary choice – neither with subservience to our inner feelings nor to external factors. To make clear and informed choices we must only see both internal and external data as signals not determinants. The resolve to act on moral grounds is repeated in the Quran.

Act, for Allah will see your actions (Al-Tawbah 9:105)

How excellent is the reward for those who are doers (Al-Imran 3:136; Al-Ankabut 29:58; Al-Zumar 39:74)

The Prophet said that through action we are led to our destiny[741] and quoted the Quran.[742]

Second, is to undertake good choice. Creative effort finds its meaning not only in the choice of good ends but also good means. The ways in which we attempt to achieve good ends must themselves be in conformance with the law and its spirit. In charity, for instance, a believer is bound by a minimum 2.5% of annual income and 30% of a final will. This avoids extreme acts that may betray other rulings designed to safeguard social and economic welfare yet leaves open so many details that are determined in accordance with concrete experience but nevertheless with a holistic view of the law.

In its third manifestation, creative effort requires the believer to distinguish between options that merely present an elementary duty and those that are more meritorious. The Quran encourages believers to seek out their best.

So give good news to My servants, those who listen to the word and follow the best of it, they are the ones whom Allah has guided, they are the people of intelligence (Al-Zumar 39:17-18)

And follow the best that has been sent down to you from your Lord (Al-Zumar 39:55)

So race with each other in all that is beneficial (Al-Ma'idah 5:48)

And the foremost are the foremost, these are nearest [to Allah] (Al-Waqi'ah 56:10-11)

The Prophet had made clear that 'God loves nobility in people's behaviour and hates baseness.'[743] This does not necessarily mean that we are to strain ourselves and our resources at all times. That would only lead to ruin. Quranic ethics emphasises moderation between the average and exceptional – all having a share of goodness.[744] The demand for the highest levels of good is an encouragement out of God's grace. Even when one's task is complete, the Quranic ethics invites the believer to strive with a longing for God.[745] Thus, morality and holiness are merged in the Quranic view. To the Prophet it states: *Truly, you conform to an exalted morality* (Al-Qalam 68:4).

Physical Effort

Any physical suffering imposed on the body as something inherently valuable or as a salutary discipline for the soul is not part of Islamic morality. Only exertion that is implied in a duty or which naturally accompanies it is accepted. The former is considered an excess and transgression as described in the Quran.[746] The Prophet warned against self-imposed hardship on several occasions saying: '… I wake and I sleep, I fast and I eat, and I marry. Whoever does not follow my example is not of me.'[747] Physical effort therefore must have meaning, that is, not simply self-inflicted pain.

Effort associated with duty is far ranging – from the effort to earn a living[748] which may be accompanied with evident joys, to the effort of self-defense and that of others which is accompanied with hardship, fear and threats.[749] It also encompasses providing help to others including the simplest act of kindness to saving a life which the Quran likens to saving all of humanity.[750] Similarly, the key acts of worship including prayer, fasting, certain charitable acts and the pilgrimage all involve physical effort. It also takes physical effort to withstand the trials that one may be subjected to during one's lifetime for purposes of spiritual elevation.

> *And We will certainly try you with something of fear and hunger and diminution of wealth and lives and productive endeavours, and give good tidings to those who persevere (Al-Baqarah 2:155)*

Action necessarily means engagement with society. While some individuals may be more greatly disposed to isolation, more comfortably practicing their faith away from the pressure of society, persistent seclusion has its moral limits. The Prophet said: 'A Muslim who mixes in society and bears its wickedness is better than one who does not mix with people and cannot tolerate them.'[751] In all cases, we have solace from people during the night,[752] in addition to taking to ourselves intermittently with complete isolation practiced in the last ten days of Ramadan.[753]

Effort and Gentleness

Earlier we noted that the Quran states:

> *Keep your duty to Allah, as much as you are able (Al-Taghabun 64:16).*

This situates action within an individual's ability. God also commands us not to kill ourselves, as He is most merciful,[754] nor to exhaust or wear ourselves out.[755] On observing a certain incident, the Prophet said: 'Truly, God rejects the torture that this man imposes upon himself....'[756] When one's circumstances compel them to break what would necessitate strict adherence under normal circumstances, the new application becomes the rule if only for a limited time. Necessity is the law.[757] This, however, does not remove obligation. It merely pardons the transgression.[758] But while giving room for this it warns against willful slackening and encourages believers toward the higher moral ground.[759]

Moderation in effort is important. The Prophet said: 'Your Lord has a right over you, your body has one; your family another, and your guests have one – give each one their rights.'[760] Strength and gentleness are thus brought together in Islam.

> *And strive hard for Allah, the verity of striving for Him: He has chosen you and placed no hardship in your religion (Al-Hajj 22:78)*

The Prophet emphasised this approach by stating 'go into it gently,[761] for whoever persists too hard in observing this law will be overcome by it (will die trying).' Gentleness, however, does not diminish from our continued effort for excellence.

The Quranic passages which command us to struggle as we must for the supreme ideal,[762] without considering our resources, do not have any other human significance. By designating this superior objective for us, and through the unlimited ennobling of our moral aspirations, they seek to propel our efforts to as high a degree as possible in their intensity. We have seen just how much the Quran encourages people to seek the best and compete with each other in their struggle for the highest ranks. The Prophet gives us the key and the motive for this noble struggle. Whereas, in the material order of things, he ordains us to content ourselves with our fate when looking at that of our fellow human beings who are less fortunate than us, in the moral order, on the contrary, he strongly recommends us always to raise our eyes towards those who are superior to us, and to try to emulate them.[763]

Conclusion

We now know what is the effort demanded by the Quran. Firstly, it is an activity, both moral and physical, which places itself at the service of a duty and which is measured by it. Secondly, it is a *clear-sighted* activity, even doubly so. Not only are its attentions turned to every available energy to be used with specific intent, but at the same time they encompass our various relationships with God, the world and ourselves so that we may apportion ourselves equitably among them, and satisfy their diverse demands. Thirdly, it is *noble* and *far-sighted*. It is not intended to consume itself instantly and remain without a result or consequence. On the contrary, it envisages a certain robustness, a certain devotion, in which joy and bliss, far from diminishing, go on to increase.

Quranic ethics emphasises moderation. This practical principle weaves itself through numerous concepts including moderation,[764] temperance,[765] generosity,[766] and gentleness in tone and attitude.[767] The Quran and Sunnah provide a concrete and recognisable measure of virtue. Within the law, each virtue has its specific value, balanced as a whole, through the general rule which commands us to harmonise our duties among them.

Regarding the degree of effort, Islam recommends a noble

attitude which comes as near as possible to perfection, accompanied by joy and hope. When the Prophet exhorted people to gentleness, he said:

> 'Go directly towards that which is just itself. Draw as near as possible, and be hopeful.'[768]

CHAPTER 6

General Conclusion

One of the noblest tasks in life is to educate people about their moral duties. The Quran does this by addressing both practice and theory. Although not directly stated, it provides all the elements that are required for people to construct a comprehensive theory of morality. Thus, it informs us of the origins of ethical rules, the conditions in which they apply, consequences which impact our attitude toward these rules, sources of inspiration, and ways to achieve virtue.

The foundation of the Quran's ethical doctrine is constituted by the five key elements of obligation, responsibility, sanction, intention and effort. In other words, it is a comprehensive system. Indeed, Quranic ethics cannot be considered solely as a religious ethics in the sense that it will only be verified in the afterlife, since it manifests in the moral conscience of human beings and through legal power, as well as requiring every individual to work toward a common order of peace and justice.

Moreover, it is not an exclusively religious ethics in the sense that it does not merely command obedience by basing its rules on human fear and hope. Rather, it takes into account the necessity and role of human reason, of its need to question, consider, comprehend, accept, and finally, adapt. The Quran justifies its commandments for precisely these reasons. Its moral teachings serve a spectrum of developmental phases. From the novice to the saint, it expresses different levels of complexity and different modes of appeal including the rational, emotional, mystical and material. Even so, these modes diminish nothing of its ultimate justification of divine wisdom.

The religious element, however, is not absent. It cannot be, for it too needs order and organisation without which we cannot hope to apply the law successfully. The guidance intended therein to illuminate certain decisions that we, given the limits of our natural light, may not be able to discern or explain rationally. Nevertheless, *ethics and religion cannot be superimposed*, and one cannot define the other.

Basic consideration reveals that from an existential point of view, the law of the conscience came before positive religious law. From our very inception, we are inspired as to what elevates and ennobles us and what debases and harms us. Every soul knows the difference between good and evil. This is something detectible in children especially as they reach an age of maturity and that continues throughout life, irrespective of belief. It is also evident in individuals who acknowledge guilt and regret their crimes, even as they lack the strength to desist from further sin.

Religious law acknowledges natural law and the inner authority that is indispensable for its establishment. Instead of nullifying ancient law, it ratifies, refines and advances it. It also acknowledges the conscience, which it not only aims to cultivate and illuminate, but upon which it relies for its continuous creative application in new realms. Essentially, it cannot be imposed on us without our acknowledgement and active reception any more than natural law. Our consent and acceptance are necessary for the transformation of divine command into moral obligation. Obedience requires belief in the obligatory nature of religious duty. *The first duty is to believe in duty*. The inner self must command obedience to divine order. In other words, faith requires commitment.

The religious and the moral are two independent notions that respond to different ideas. The religious notion responds to an ideal of *Being*, while the moral responds to one of *Becoming*. In the first instance, the ideal is a perfect being, the true and the beautiful in itself, an object of knowledge, contemplation and love; in the second, the ideal is the perfect work called virtue, an object of aspiration and creation. It is we who bring these concepts together as we recognise in the Creator attributes which are properly moral, such as justice, wisdom and goodness; we even make His legislation ours; we call His order 'our order', without which the two notions would remain separate.

Finally, by not specifying the quantitative dimensions of most of its commands the Quran reinforces and legitimises trust in the common conscience. Moreover, it draws attention to the necessity of such trust for its just application due to its dependence on human potential, concrete circumstances and the prioritisation of duties at any given moment. In doing so, it grants every individual conscience a role in the legislative action, a part which is necessary for formulating our concrete duty at every moment. This is how the Quran eases and facilitates respect of its commands. The religious element must therefore follow the natural element and in so doing become a properly moral effort. Indeed, the religious aspect is only one element within an extensive synthesis.

That said, this doctrine may be called a *religious ethics* at one critical juncture, namely, *intentionality*. Here, the religious sense is clear and irreplaceable. The aim of our acts of obedience must be none other than God. We cannot act for or in the name of any other aim since that renders the act worthless. This does not mean that we cannot pursue material and moral well-being for itself or as a duty or right, but not as a reward for obedience.

Thus, if we consider the purpose for which the will acts as the defining characteristic of an ethical doctrine, then Quranic ethics is a religious ethics. For this ethics neither pleasure, nor usefulness, nor happiness, nor perfection can themselves constitute its principle. Everything must be subordinated to the authority of *Duty* in the most sacred, real and sublime sense of the word.

In this moral system, the most profound notion in which all commandments may be summed is *taqwa*, or heedfulness. Heedfulness being the deepest respect for the law. From this perspective, duty is positioned in the emotional realm. Respect finds its expression between the two extreme feelings of hope and fear both to encourage and control, to support our quest for modesty, which is how the Prophet defined the heart of Quranic ethics. Therefore, this ethics galvanizes all the modes and powers of moral life and brings them back to their point of equilibrium even while aiming for the highest ideal.

Quranic ethics reconciles our *freedom* with the *discipline* of our will. Its partially flexible and partially fixed nature allows adaptation to diverse contexts without yielding to superficial elements and whims. The law clearly distinguishes between the innate tendencies and temporary needs, whether legitimate or illegitimate; between that which is immutable and that which can be entrusted to individual judgment since it varies according to context and capacity; and that which is to be corrected or eliminated. It is in order to take these aspects into account that it has established the threefold principle of what is *prescribed*, *permitted* and *prohibited*.

All ethical rules in the Quran contain a double imperative: to perform a *duty* and realise a *good*, or rather to perform an *essential duty* and a *duty of perfection*. No compromise is admitted in the performance of one's essential duties. With regard to the duty of perfection, however, there is greater leeway as the Quran uses exhortation and encouragement as opposed to binding command. The path from the essential duty to the perfect duty, which presents itself to the initiative and valor of each individual, is marked by greater degrees of merit. Each step is blessed, inviting believers to aspire to higher and higher heights.

One can conclude that the Quranic theory of morality permits its comprehension and application in any time and place. Quranic ethics is absolutely complete in itself. It is an 'integral ethics'.

Notes

1 *Translated from Draz, Muhammad Abdallah (1951). La Moral du Koran. Paris: Presses Universitaires de France. p. xxiv*

2 *Ibid. p. xxv*

3 Keep in mind that Draz finished this work in 1947. Nevertheless, the critique that he levels against 19th Century works largely remain valid up to this day.

4 Quran 43:22-23

5 Quran 91:7-8

6 Quran 75:14

7 Quran 79:40

8 Quran 17:70

9 Quran 2:34

10 Quran 7:11; 14:29; 20;116; 38:72 etc.

11 Quran 95:4

12 Quran 70:19-22

13 Quran 70:5

14 Quran 7:179

15 Quran 91:9-10

16 Quran 4:1; 49:13

17 Quran 49:12

18 Quran 67:14

19 Quran 24:35
20 Quran 6:57; 12:40; 6:62
21 Quran 4:128
22 Quran 17:35
23 Quran 24:30
24 See for instance Quran 49:6; 2:282; 5;100; 7:26; 2:269; 7:28; 16:90
25 Quran 6:19; 7:158; 25:1
26 Quran 2:44, 267; 83:1-3
27 Quran 4:135
28 Quran 3:75-6
29 Quran 5:2, 8
30 Quran 24:49-50
31 Quran 3:134
32 Quran 9:120
33 Quran 9:81
34 Quran 33:36
35 Quran 2:256, 4:80; 10:99; 88:21-22; 24:54
36 Malik, *Muwatta, Kitab al-Jami', Bab* 13.
37 Al-Bukhari, *Sahih, Kitab al-Adab, Bab* 76.
38 Quran 73:20
39 Quran 4:43
40 Quran 16:67
41 Quran 16:67
42 Quran 2:219
43 Quran 4:43
44 Quran 5:90
45 Quran 2:184, 219; 25:64
46 Quran 2:237
47 Quran 2:280
48 Quran 42:41-43
49 Quran 2:158
50 Al Bukhari, *Sahih, Kitab al-Iman, Bab* 6
51 Quran 33:5
52 Al-Bukhari, *Sahih, Kitab al-Iman, Bab* 39

53 Al-Bukhari, *Kitab al-Buyu'*, title of *Bab* 3
54 Cf. Ahmad, al-Musnad via *Wabissa*. See also Muslim, *Sahih, Kitab al-Birr', Bab* 5.
55 Quran 5:7; 57:8
56 Al-Bukhari, *Sahih, 'Kitab al-Nudhur', Bab* 27
57 Al-Bukhari, *Sahih, 'Kitab al-Ijara', Bab* 15
58 Al-Bukhari, *Sahih, 'Kitab al-Shurut', Bab* 13
59 Ibn Majah, *Sunan, 'Kitab al-Ahkam', Bab* 23
60 Quran 4:58
61 Ibid.
62 Al-Bukhari, *Sahih, 'Kitab al-Ahkam', Bab* 3
63 Ahmad, *Musnad*, via 'Imran ibn Husayn
64 Quran 17:14-15; 81:14; 82:5
65 Quran 18:47-9
66 Quran 2:283
67 Quran 17:36; 102:8
68 Al-Tirmidhi, *Sunan, 'Kitab Sifat al-Qiyama', Bab* 1
69 Al-Bukhari, *Sahih, 'Kitab al-Wasiyya', Bab* 9
70 Quran 2:134, 141
71 Quran 20:122
72 Quran 12:79
73 Quran 52:21
74 Quran 16:25
75 Quran 2:166-67; 7:38-39; 34:31-2; 40:47-8; 43:36-9
76 Muslim, *Sahih, 'Kitab al-Wasiyyah', Bab* 3
77 Muslim, *Sahih, 'Kitab al-Zakat', Bab* 20
78 Quran 5:32
79 Quran 5:79
80 Quran 7:165; 6:47
81 Muslim, *Sahih, 'Kitab al-Birr'*, Bab 7
82 Quran 7:156
83 Quran 4:165
84 Quran 7:172-3
85 Quran 6:130-1; 26:208-9
86 Abu Dawud, Sunan, *'Kitab al-Hudud', Bab* 17; al-Bukhari,

Sahih, Kitab al-muharibin min ahl al-kufr wa'l-ridda, Bab 8

87 Muslim, *Sahih, 'Kitab al-Iman', Bab* 54

88 Quran 2:286

89 Quran 5:89

90 See also Quran 2:286

91 Quran 91:8-10

92 Quran 31: end

93 Quran 90:10-18

94 Quran 31:4

95 Quran 91:9-10

96 Quran 14:22; 74:37

97 Quran 7:176; 37:69-70

98 Quran 39:62

99 Quran 56:58-9

100 Quran 56:63-4

101 Al-Bukhari, *Sahih, 'Kitab Bad' al-Khalq', Bab* 20; Muslim, *Sahih, 'Kitab al-Iman', Bab* 7.

102 Quran 12:34

103 Quran 12:24

104 Quran 17:74; 48:26; 28:10; 49:7

105 Quran 9:25

106 Quran 2:128; 27:19; 19:32; 3:7; 12:33, 53; 114:1-4; 1:4-5

107 Quran 48:26

108 Quran 6:53

109 Quran 48:18

110 Quran 43:36; 8:23

111 Quran 2:26

112 Quran 42:13

113 Quran 6:149

114 Quran 16:93

115 Cf. al-Bukhari, *Sahih, 'Kitab al-Mussaqat',Bab* 4; *'Kitab al-Diyat', Bab* 28

116 See al-Bukhari, *Sahih, 'Kitab al-Ahkam'*, Bab 19

117 Quran 4:92

118 Quran 21:78-9

119 Ibn Rushd, *Bidaya*, vol. 2, p. 348
120 Quran 4:92
121 Al-Amir, *al-Majmu'*, vol. 2, p. 372
122 Quran 9:60
123 Quran 24:31; 66:8
124 Quran 3:25
125 Quran 4:18
126 Quran 4:17; 3:135
127 Quran 5:93
128 Quran 2:185; 18:24
129 Al-Bukhari, *Sahih, 'Kitab al-Mazalim', Bab* 10; *'Kitab al-Riqaq', 'Bab al-Qisas'*
130 Muslim, *Sahih, 'Kitab al-Birr', Bab* 15
131 Ahmad, *Musnad*, through 'Aisha
132 Quran 8:38
133 Quran 8:33, 39:53-4; 42:25
134 Quran 83:7; 18
135 Quran 29:45
136 Quran 9:103
137 Quran 2:183
138 Quran 70:19-34
139 Quran 5:91
140 Quran 16:105
141 Quran 83:14
142 Quran 8:29
143 Quran 91:9-10
144 Al-Bukhari, *Sahih, 'Kitab al-Hudud', Bab* 12; Malik, *Muwatta, 'Kitab al-Hudud', Bab* 9; Abu Dawud, quoted by al-Suyuti, *al-Jami'*
145 Quran 24:2
146 Al-Bukhari, *Sahih, 'Kitab al-'Ilm', Bab* 9
147 Quran 49:12
148 Al-Bukhari, *Sahih, 'Kitab al-Iman', Bab* 10
149 Malik, *Muwatta, 'Kitab al-Hudud', Bab* 1
150 Ibn Hazm, *al-Muhalla*, vol. 11, p. 153

151 Muslim, *Sahih, 'Kitab al-Hudud'*, *Bab* 51
152 Quran 2:275; 4:7, 11, 12, 24 twice, 103; 9:60; 58:3; 60:10
153 Quran 33:36
154 Quran 4:66
155 Ibid
156 Quran 4:11, 12, 24; 9:60; 60:10
157 Quran 6:90; 12:104; 23:72; 38:86; 42:23; 42:40; 68:46
158 Quran 2:256; 3:20; 5:92, 99; 6:90; 10:99, 108; 13:40; 16:82; 38:87; 39:41; 42:48; 43:44; 64:12; 68:52; 69:48; 74:54; 76:29; 80;11; 81:27; 88:21-22
159 Quran 21:5; 27:224; 36:69; 37:36; 69:41; 52:30
160 Quran 52:29; 69:42
161 Quran 21:5
162 Quran 7:184; 23:70; 34:8, 46; 37:36; 44:14; 52;29; 68:2, 51; 81:22
163 Quran 26:210; 81:25
164 Quran 7:203; 10:15, 37, 38; 11:13, 35; 12:111
165 Quran 53:3
166 Quran 4:174; 5:15; 6:104, 122; 7:157, 203; 13:16; 14:1; 24:35, 40; 33:46; 35:20; 39:22; 42:52; 45:20; 57:9; 64:8
167 Quran 2:2, 5, 97, 137, 150; 3:20, 103, 138; 6:157; 7:52, 158, 203; 9:18, 33; 10:57, 108; 12:111; 16:64, 89, 102; 20:135; 24:54; 27:2, 77; 28:49, 85; 31:3, 5; 32:3; 33:4; 34:24; 39:18; 41:44; 43:24; 45:11, 20; 48:28; 53:22, 23, 30; 61:9; 68:7; 93:7; 96:11
168 Quran 1:5; 2:256; 3:101; 4:46; 6:39, 126, 153, 161; 16:76; 17:9; 18:1; 20:135; 22:67; 23:73; 24:46; 3:30; 36, 61; 39:28; 42:52; 43:43, 61; 46:30; 67:22; 72:2; 81:28; 98:3,5
169 Quran 39:23
170 Quran 15:27
171 Quran 73:5; 86:13, 14
172 Quran 30:30
173 Quran 16:9
174 Quran 2:135; 3:95; 4:26; 6:90; 16:123; 21:92; 23:52; 37:37; 42:13

175 Quran 6:115; 16:76

176 Quran 2:26, 91, 109, 119, 213; 3:60, 62, 108; 4:105, 170; 5:48, 83, 84; 6:5, 66, 114, 115; 7:181; 8:6, 7, 8;9:33; 10:35, 53, 94, 108; 11:17, 102; 13:1, 19; 16:102; 17:81, 105; 18:29, 56; 19:34; 21:18; 22:6, 62; 23:70, 90; 28:48, 53; 31:30; 32:3; 33:4; 34:6, 48, 49; 35, 24, 31;37:37; 39:2, 41; 40:5; 41:42, 53; 42:17, 24; 43:30, 78; 45:6; 46:7, 30; 47:2, 3; 48:28; 50:5; 51:23; 61:9; 69:51

177 Quran 6:57, 157; 11:17; 27:79; 29:49; 40:66; 47:14; 57:9;65:11; 98:1, 4

178 Quran 2:129, 151, 282; 3:164; 4:113, 116; 11:14; 20:114; 62:2

179 Quran 2:129, 151, 231, 269; 3:164; 4:113; 10:1; 17:39; 31:2; 33:34; 43:4; 54:5; 62:2

180 Quran 2:256; 31:22

181 Quran 10:57; 17:82; 41:44

182 Quran 2:129, 151; 3:164; 62:2; 80:3; 91:9

183 Quran 6:122; 8:24; 25:22

184 Quran 9:122; 16:43; 21:7

185 Quran 90:11-17

186 Quran 33:21; 46:35; 60:4; 61:14

187 Quran 17:110; 25:67

188 Quran 42:15

189 Quran 2:148; 3:114; 5:48; 23:61

190 Quran 11:7; 18:9; 67:2

191 Quran 17:53

192 Quran 4:171; 9:119; 39:33

193 Quran 24:30, 31, 33; 33:32, 33; 70:29-30; 74:4

194 Quran 2:168, 172; 5:4, 5; 16:114

195 Quran 2:177; 18:28; 74:7

196 Quran 25:63

197 Quran 4:94; 49:6, 12

198 Quran 16:90

199 Quran 6:151; 17:23; 19:8; 46:15

200 Quran 17:23-34

201 Quran 2:229, 231; 4:19; 65:2

202 Quran 2:233; 65:6
203 Quran 2:233; 236; 65:7
204 Quran2:229, 236, 241; 33:49
205 Quran 2:177, 16:90; 17:26
206 Quran 4:36
207 Quran 2:177; 16:90; 17:26
208 Quran 2:177; 4:36; 9:60; 17:26; 70:24-25
209 Quran 2:267; 3:92
210 Quran 90:14-16
211 Quran 2:177; 9:60; 90:13
212 Quran 2:282; 6:152; 17:35
213 Quran 13:22
214 Quran 2:282, 13:22; 4:58, 127,135; 5:8; 6:152; 7:29; 19:90; 42:15; 57:25
215 Quran 17:35; 55:7-9
216 Quran 2:282, 283; 65:2
217 Quran 4:135; 6:152
218 Quran 2:283; 4:48; 70:32
219 Quran 2:177; 5:1; 13:20; 70:32. Notice above all, with what insistence and precision the Quran commands this duty in international relations: *Do not use your oaths to deceive each other... just because one party may be more numerous than another. Allah tests you with this* (16:92).
220 Quran 59:9
221 Quran 7:199; 24:22; 25:63, 72
222 Quran 13:22; 23:96
223 Quran 3:104, 110, 114; 7:157, 199
224 Quran 9:71
225 Quran 4:114
226 Quran 4:114
227 Quran 5:2
228 Quran 90:17
229 Quran 3:103
230 Quran 13:21
231 Quran 59:9

232 Quran 59:10
233 Quran 16:125
234 Quran 2:228, 232, 233, 234, 235, 240, 263; 4:5, 8, 114; 33:32
235 Quran 2:177; 6:163
236 Quran 24:54
237 Quran 7:185; 30:8; 38:29
238 Quran 33:41
239 Quran 16:78; 28:73; 43:12-14; 56:63-64
240 9:129; 39:38
241 Quran 18:23
242 Quran 2:165; 5:54
243 Quran 2:21; 51:56
244 Quran 2:263; 4:48, 59, 128; 7:26; 9:120; 17:35
245 Quran 2:177, 189, 269; 3:92
246 Quran 2:221; 4:19
247 Quran 4:125; 5:50; 41:33
248 Quran 2:282; 33:5
249 Quran 29:45
250 Quran 2:177; 22:32; 29:33; 49:3
251 Quran 2:236
252 Quran 3:123; 17:24; 46:15; 56:70; 106:3-4
253 Quran 2:180, 241
254 Quran 3:186; 42:43; 46:35
255 Quran 4:75
256 Quran 4:9
257 Quran 4:94; 93:6-11
258 Quran 14:22
259 Quran 2:232, 5:6; 9:103; 33:33, 53; 58:12
260 Quran 2:232; 9:103; 24:28, 30; 92:18
261 Quran 73:6
262 Quran 2:265; 4:66
263 Quran 13:28; 39:23
264 Quran 2:282
265 Quran 29:45
266 Quran 2:183, 187, 237; 5:8

267 Quran 49:6
268 Quran 25:71
269 Quran 5:100
270 Quran 2:177; 8:74; 9:44; 24:62; 29:3, 11; 49:15; 58:22; 59:8
271 Quran 5:82, 83; 32:15
272 Quran 3:7; 4:162; 13:43; 29:43, 49; 30:22; 34:6 35:28; 39:9
273 Quran 2:164, 269; 3:7; 6:97 , 98, 105, 151, 152; 7:32; 9:11; 10:5, 24; 13:3, 4, 19; 16:11,12, 13, 67, 69; 30:21, 23, 24, 28; 38:29; 39:9, 18, 21, 42; 45:5
274 Quran 36:70
275 Quran 6:50, 104; 11:24; 12:108; 13:16; 24:44; 35:19; 40:58
276 Quran 2:186; 49:7; 72:14
277 Quran 68:4
278 Quran 3:110; 98:7
279 Quran 4:29
280 Quran 4:24, 25; 5:5; 17:32; 25:68
281 Quran 4:25; 5:5; 24:33
282 Quran 6:151; 7:33; 16:90
283 Quran 22:30
284 Quran 4:49; 53:32
285 Quran 4:135
286 Quran 3:156; 8:47; 33:69
287 Quran 4:32; 15:88; 18:28
288 Quran 89:19-20
289 Quran 17:37
290 Quran 4:2; 74:5
291 Quran 4:2; 74:5
292 Quran 6:151; 17:31
293 Quran 17:23
294 Quran2:229, 231, 232, 233; 4:19; 65:6
295 Quran 6:151; 17:33; 25:68
296 Quran 2:11; 7:56
297 Quran 5:2; 7:33; 16:90
298 Quran 2:188; 4:29
299 Quran 4:6; 6:152; 17:34

300 Quran 107:2
301 Quran 93:9
302 Quran 89:17
303 Quran 89:18; 107:3
304 Quran 93:10
305 Quran 2:267
306 Quran 74:6
307 Quran 49:17
308 Quran 25:72
309 Quran 8:27
310 Quran 24:27-28, 58-59, 61
311 Quran 24:62
312 Quran 49:12
313 Quran 49:12
314 Quran 49:11
315 Quran 49:11
316 Quran 5:2
317 Quran 3:103
318 Quran 59:19
319 Quran 6:136
320 Quran 33:36
321 Quran 2:22; 18:end
322 Quran 2:224; 5:89; 6:108
323 Quran 1:7; 2:16, 108, 175; 3:90, 164; 4:44, 60, 116, 136, 167, 176; 5:12; 6:39, 56, 116, 119, 140, 144; 7:179; 10:45, 108; 14:3; 18:104; 19:38; 22:4, 12; 25:42, 44; 28:50, 85; 30:29; 31:11; 33:36; 34:24; 36:62; 39:22; 41:52; 42:18; 43:40; 46:5, 32; 53:30; 54:47; 60:1; 62:2; 667:29; 68:7
324 Quran 7:179, 205
325 Quran 2:17; 6:39, 22; 13:16; 14:1; 24:40; 35:20; 57:9; 65:11
326 Quran 4:27, 135; 23:74; 27:60
327 Quran 4:22; 17:32
328 Quran 9:37; 18:104; 35:8; 43:37; 47:14; 19:11
329 Quran 67:22
330 Quran 22:31

331 Quran 6:119; 7:176; 18:28; 28:50; 30:29; 42:15; 47:14, 16
332 Quran 25:43; 45:23
333 Quran 2:90, 102; 3:187; 18:50
334 Quran 4:38; 17:27; 22:13
335 Quran 2:168, 208; 7:27; 18:50; 35:6
336 Quran 49:11
337 Quran 4:140; 5:51
338 Quran 7:176, 177, 179; 25:44; 62:5
339 Quran 49:12
340 Quran 2:17, 18, 171; 6:50, 104; 11:24; 13:16, 19; 22:46; 27:81; 28:72; 30:53; 32:27; 35:19; 40:58; 41:44; 43:40
341 Quran 2:18, 171; 6:39; 7:100, 179; 8:22; 10:42; 11:24; 21:45; 25:44; 27:80; 28:71; 30:52; 41:, 44; 43:40
342 Quran 2:102, 103; 6:35, 37, 111; 16:101; 21:24; 27:61; 28:57; 30:30, 59; 31:25; 34:28, 36; 39:9, 29, 49, 64; 40:57; 45:26; 63:8
343 Quran 2:44, 171; 3:65; 4:78; 5:58, 103; 7:179; 8:22; 9:81, 127; 23:80; 25:44; 29:63; 36:62; 49:4; 59:13, 14; 63:7
344 Quran 53:30
345 Quran30:7
346 Quran 10:39; 27:84
347 Quran 3:66; 22:3, 8; 31:20
348 Quran 2:80, 169; 4:157; 6:100, 108, 119, 140, 143, 144, 148; 7:28, 33; 10:68; 17:5; 22:71; 24:15; 30:29; 31:6; 43:20; 45:24; 46:4; 53:28
349 Quran 3:151; 7:33; 21:24; 22:71; 27:64; 37:156; 40:35; 53:23
350 Quran 18:51; 37:150; 43:19
351 Quran 6:136; 16:59
352 Quran 42:16
353 Quran 5:68
354 Quran 9:109
355 Quran 29:41
356 Quran 2:170; 3:154; 5:77, 104; 9:30; 33:33; 37:69, 70; 43:22
357 Quran 2:78; 4:157; 6:116, 1438; 10:36, 66; 43:20; 45:24, 32; 53:23, 28

358 Quran 8:8; 16:72; 17:81; 18:56; 21:18; 22:62; 25:4; 24:67; 31:30; 34:49; 40:5; 42:24; 47:3 58:2
359 Quran 10:66; 19:42
360 Quran 9:30; 13:33; 33:4; 53:23, 27
361 Quran 3:37, 78; 4:50; 5:103; 6:112, 137, 140; 18:5; 23;90; 29:3, 12, 17; 37:86, 151, 152
362 Quran 5:90
363 Quran 2:256; 68:6
364 Quran 2:13, 130; 6:140
365 Quran 4:171; 5:77; 6:108; 11:112; 16:9; 18:28; 23:7; 70:31; 72:4
366 Quran 2:169; 5:62, 63, 79; 9:9; 17:38; 63:2
367 Quran 2:169, 268; 4:22; 7:28; 17:32; 24:21
368 Quran 9:67; 24:21; 58:2
369 Quran 4:22; 40:10
370 Quran 2:282; 3:82; 5:3, 59, 81; 6:121, 145; 9:8, 67; 24:4, 55; 57:16, 26, 27; 59:19
371 Quran 2:40, 145, 229, 254' 3:94; 5:107; 6:21, 52, 93, 144, 157; 7:37; 9:23; 10:17, 106; 11:18; 18:50, 57; 19:38; 24:50; 25:4; 19:49, 68; 30:29; 31:11; 32:22; 39:32; 49:11; 60:9; 61:7
372 Quran 2:231; 4:97; 7:177; 10:23, 44; 35:32; 65:1
373 Quran 2:217; 17:40; 18:5; 19:89; 24:15; 33:35
374 Quran 2:88; 4:2, 20, 48, 50, 112; 5:106; 17:31; 33:58; 49:12
375 Quran 2:283
376 Quran 2:187
377 Quran 5:41
378 Quran 5:90; 9:28, 95, 125
379 Quran 20:115
380 Quran 9:45, 110; 24:50
381 Quran 4:72-73
382 Quran 24:48-49
383 Quran 2:274; 6:43; 22:53; 57:16
384 Quran 25:21; 40:56
385 Quran 26:225
386 Quran 26:226

387 Quran 7:176
388 Quran 5:91
389 Quran 83:14; 91:10
390 Quran 2:10; 5:52; 9:25; 12:53; 24:50; 47:20
391 Quran 6:122; 27:80; 30:52; 35:22
392 Quran 8:22, 55; 95:6; 98:6
393 Quran 13:12; 50:17,18
394 Quran 50:16
395 Al-Bukhari, *Sahih, 'Kitab al-Iman', Bab* 38
396 Quran 2:149, 233, 234, 237, 244; 4:1, 33, 58; 5:7, 8; 8:39, 72; 9:16, 105; 11:123; 24:28, 29, 30, 60; 25:20; 29:45; 33:34, 54, 55; 58:3, 13; 59:18; 63:11
397 Quran 2:181, 326, 224, 227, 231, 283; 3:156; 4:94, 135, 148; 11:112; 16:91; 33:1, 2, 52; 49:1
398 Cf. al-Tirmidhi, quoted by Ibn Dayba', *Taysir, 'Kitab al-Haya", Bab* 1
399 Quran 12:24
400 Quran 2:74, 77, 140, 144; 3:63, 98, 99, 167; 4:63, 108; 5:61, 71; 8:47; 9:78; 10:36; 11:5; 17:47; 21:4; 23:96; 24:53; 25:58; 27:93; 29:10; 35:8; 36:76; 42:6; 46:8; 49:18; 90:7
401 Quran 17:29
402 Quran 4:102
403 Quran 4:84
404 Quran 2:251
405 Quran 22:40
406 Quran 9:14
407 Quran 3:144, 145; 6:120, 138, 147; 11:3, 111; 12:110; 32:22; 45:22; 46:19; 53:31, 41
408 Quran 9:111
409 Al-Bukhari, *Sahih, 'Kitab al-Murda', Bab* 19
410 Quran 16:32
411 For the good: 2:210; 3:148; 4:134; 12:56, 57; 16:30, 41, 97, 122; 29:27; 41:31. For the bad: 2:85, 114; 3:12, 56; 5:41; 9:74; 17:75; 22:9, 1; 24:19; 32:21; 39:26, 40; 41:16; 71:25
412 Quran 39:10

413 Quran 16:112
414 Quran 18:35-42
415 Quran 68:24-33
416 Quran 11:102; 17:16 with those not guilty removed or protected by God.
417 Quran 54:43
418 Quran 6:6; 30:9; 35:44; 40:21, 82; 46:26
419 Quran 17:68, 69
420 Quran 7:97, 98
421 Quran 16:46
422 Quran 16:45; 67:16
423 Quran 16:47
424 Quran 3:120; 22:38; 8:19
425 Quran 2:194; 9:36, 123
426 Quran 61:13; 37:171-3; 58:21
427 Quran 3:139
428 Quran 3:12; 8:36; 54:45
429 Quran 58:20
430 Quran 9:2; 59:5
431 Quran 47:11
432 Quran 39:69
433 Quran 64:11
434 Quran 2:257; 5:16; 33:43; 65:11
435 Quran 4:68, 175; 5:16; 10:10; 22:54
436 Quran 33:71
437 Quran 8:29
438 Quran 57:28
439 Quran 47:2
440 Quran 21:76; 47;17
441 Quran 48:4, 18
442 Quran 16:104; 3:86; 5:51; 6:144; 9:19, 100; 46:10; 61:7; 62:5; 5:108; 9:24, 80; 68:6; 61:5; 5:67; 9:37; 16:107; 39:3; 40:42
443 Quran 14:27; 40:34; 45:23; 61:5
444 Quran 5:13
445 Quran 2:6; 4:155; 7:101; 9:87, 93; 10:74; 16:108; 18:57;

40:35; 45:23; 63:3
446 Quran 47:23
447 Quran 2:10
448 Quran 2:15
449 Quran 9:77
450 Quran 59:19
451 Quran 43:36
452 Quran 2:257
453 Quran 17:86; 42:24
454 Quran 2:152
455 Quran 3:162, 174
456 Quran 39:7
457 Quran 58:22
458 Quran 16:128; 29:69
459 Quran 7:196, 45:19
460 Quran 49:13
461 Quran 2:205; 5:64
462 Quran 61:3
463 Quran 35:39
464 Quran 40:35
465 Quran 42:16
466 Quran 8:6-7; 16:106
467 Quran 2:88, 89, 90, 159, 161; 3:162; 4:52; 5:80; 33:57, 61, 64; 40:52; 47:23; 48:6
468 Quran 4:93
469 Quran 13:25
470 Quran 24:23
471 Quran 8:16
472 Quran 42:30
473 Quran 3:186
474 Quran 3:153
475 Quran 18:108
476 Quran 35:36
477 Quran 2:124; 3:140, 141, 142, 152, 166; 9:16; 21:35; 29:2, 3; 30:41; 32:21; 47:31

478 Quran 2:214; 3:185; 4:124; 9:21, 111; 11:23, 108; 18:107; 22:5-6; 23:22; 25:15; 26:90; 31:8; 32:19; 39:73; 40:8; 41:30; 42:7; 46:14, 16; 47:6; 50:31; 59:20; 68:34; 79:41; 81:13; 89:30. Hell 2:39, 81, 167, 206, 217, 257, 275; 3:12, 116, 131, 151, 162, 196; 4:10, 14, 30, 93, 97, 115, 121, 140, 169; 5:10, 37, 72, 86; 6:128; 7:18, 36; 8:14, 16, 36, 37; 9:17, 49, 63, 68, 73, 95, 113; 10:8; 11:16, 17, 98, 113, 119; 13:18, 35; 14:29, 30; 16:29, 62; 17:63; 18:100, 102, 106; 19:72, 86; 21:29; 22:4, 51, 72; 24, 57; 25:65; 26:91; 29:25, 68; 32:13; 33:64; 34:42; 36:63; 38:27, 85; 39:8, 32, 60, 71, 72; 40:6, 48, 76; 41:19, 24, 28; 42:7; 43:74; 45:34; 46:34; 47:12; 48:6, 13; 50:24; 51:13; 57:15, 19; 58:8; 59:3; 64:10; 66:9, 10; 72:23; 79:39; 81:12; 82:14; 83:16; 84:12; 87:12; 92:14; 98:6; 111:3

479 Quran 2:97, 223; 9:112; 10:64; 22:34, 37; 27:2; 39:17; 46:12

480 Quran 4:104; 18:46; 35:29

481 Quran 4:95; 18:46; 35:29

482 Quran 23:111; 24:52; 33:71; 40:51

483 Quran 33:47

484 Quran 2:143; 3:171, 195

485 Quran 3:115; 21:94

486 Quran 2:158; 4:147; 17:19; 42:23; 64:17

487 Quran 2:5, 289; 3:104, 130; 5:90; 7:8, 157; 8:45; 22:77; 23:1, 102; 298:31, 51; 28:67; 30:38; 31:5; 59:9; 62:10; 64:16; 87:14; 91:9

488 Quran 3:14; 4:59; 11:49; 13:29; 17:35; 19:76; 20:132; 28:83; 43:35

489 Quran2:184, 197, 271, 280; 3:110; 4:25, 46, 170; 9:3, 41, 74; 16:126; 18:46; 19:76; 22:30; 24:27, 60; 29:16; 30:38; 47:21; 64:16

490 Quran 2:110; 3:30; 94:7

491 Quran 42:23; 73:20

492 Quran 2:272; 3:57; 4:173; 8:60; 20:112; 35:30; 39:10; 49:14; 72:13

493 Quran 2:245, 261; 4:40; 30:39; 34:37; 57:18; 64:17

494 Quran 16:96-7; 24:38

495 Quran 4:40, 173; 10:26; 30:45; 42:26

496 Quran 2:61, 112, 262, 274, 277; 3:199; 4:100, 152; 7:170; 9:120; 11:115; 42:40; 47:36; 57:19

497 Quran 3:172, 179; 4:67, 74, 114, 146, 162; 17:9; 18:2; 22:58; 33:29, 35, 44; 35:7; 48:10, 16; 49:3; 62:7; 65:5; 67:12

498 Quran 2:103; 27:89; 28:84

499 Quran 8:4, 74; 22:50; 24:26; 33:31, 44; 39:4; 36:11; 57:18

500 Quran 41:8; 68:3; 84:25; 95:6

501 Quran 4:31; 22:59

502 Quran 101:7

503 Quran 82:13

504 Quran 26:277; 28:61; 43:83; 46:12; 50:45; 99:8

505 Quran 2:7, 10, 79, 85, 90, 104, 114, 162, 165, 174, 178, 196, 211; 3:4, 21, 56, 77, 88, 91, 105, 106, 176, 177, 178, 188; 4:18, 37, 102, 138, 151, 161, 173; 5:2, 32, 36, 73, 80, 94, 95; 6:49, 93, 147, 157, 160; 8:25; 9:3, 61, 74, 79, 90, 101; 10;15, 27, 52, 70; 11:3; 12:110; 13:25, 34; 14:2, 22; 16:63, 88, 94, 104, 106, 117; 17:10; 18:2; 19:37, 79; 20:127; 22:18, 25, 57; 24:11, 19, 23, 63; 25:19, 27, 69; 26:213; 27:5; 28:64, 84; 29:23; 30:16; 31:6, 7, 24; 32:22; 33:8, 30, 57, 73; 34:5, 8, 38; 35:7, 10; 37:33, 38; 38:26; 39:13, 26, 47, 54, 55; 41:6, 27, 50; 42:16, 21, 26, 42, 45; 43:39, 65; 45:7, 8, 9, 10, 11; 46:20; 48:16, 17; 51:60; 52:7, 45; 57:13, 20; 58:4, 5, 15, 16; 59:4, 7, 15; 64:5; 65:10; 67:28; 68:33; 70:1; 72:17; 76:31; 77:15, 19, 24, 28, 34, 37, 40, 45, 47, 49; 83:1; 84:24; 88:24; 107:4

506 Cf. al-Bukhari, *Sahih, 'Ba'ad al-Khalq'*, Bab 7

507 Quran 2:38, 62, 112, 262, 274, 277; 3:170; 5:69; 6:48; 7:35, 49; 10:62; 15:46; 27:89; 34:37; 41:30, 40; 43:63; 44:55; 46:13

508 Quran 2:38, 62, 112, 262, 274, 277; 3:170; 5:69; 6:48; 7:35, 49; 10:62; 21:103; 35:34; 39:81; 41:30; 43:68; 46:13

509 Quran 66:8

510 Quran 2:268, 271; 3:133, 136, 157, 195; 4:31, 129; 5:9, 65; 8:4, 29, 74; 11:11; 24:22, 26; 29:7; 33:35, 71; 34:4; 35:7; 36:11; 39:35; 40:7; 42:25; 46:16, 31; 47:2; 48:5, 29; 49:3; 57:20, 21, 28; 61:12; 64:9, 17; 65:5; 66:8; 67:12

511 Quran 2:218; 3:107, 132, 157; 4:129, 175; 6:155; 7:57, 204; 9:21, 71, 99; 10:58; 19:85; 24:56; 27:46; 36:58; 42:8; 43:32; 45:30; 49:10; 57:13; 76:31
512 Quran 7:45; 15:47; 19:96; 43:67
513 Quran 75:23
514 Quran 30:15; 43:70; 76:11; 80:39; 84:9
515 Quran 17:79; 37:42; 70:35
516 Quran 3:106; 75:22; 76:11; 80:38; 83:24; 88:8
517 Quran 2:212; 83:29
518 Quran 57:12, 19; 66:8
519 Quran 4:69; 29:9; 89:29
520 Quran 13:23; 36:56; 40:8; 43:70; 52:21
521 See also Quran 39:73
522 Quran 13:23, 24
523 Quran 10:2
524 Quran 33:44; 36:58
525 Quran 55:11
526 Quran 4:96; 8:4; 9:20; 58:11
527 Quran 54:55
528 Quran 3:15; 57:20
529 Quran 5:119; 9:100; 58:22; 89:28; 92:21; 98:8
530 Quran 88:9
531 Quran 7:43, 44; 39:74
532 Quran 19:62; 56:25; 88:11
533 Quran 10:10; 19:23; 19:62; 25:75; 56:26
534 Quran 10:10
535 Quran 44:56
536 Quran 39:61; 40:7, 9; 44:56; 46:31; 52:18, 27; 61:10; 66:6; 76:11;92:17
537 Quran 21:101-102
538 Quran 15:48; 35:35; 56:89
539 Quran 15:46; 50:34; 56:91
540 Quran 6:127; 10:25
541 Quran 3:133; 57:21
542 Quran 39:74

543 Quran 4:57; 13:35; 36:56; 76:14; 77:41
544 Quran 76:31
545 Quran 25:24
546 Quran 54:54
547 Quran 47:15
548 Quran 15:45; 44:52; 55:50, 66; 56:31; 77:41; 88:12
549 Quran 76:5, 17; 83:27
550 Quran 36:57; 47:15; 55:68; 77:42; 78:32
551 Quran 55:54; 69:23; 76:14
552 Quran 13:35; 56:33
553 Quran 56:33
554 Quran 9:72; 61:12
555 Quran 25:75; 29:58; 34:37; 39:20; 69:22; 88:10
556 Quran 2:25; 3:15, 136, 195, 198; 4:13, 57, 122; 5:85; 7:43; 9:72, 89; 10:9; 14:22; 16:31; 18:31; 22:14, 23; 29:58; 47:12; 48:5, 17; 57:12; 58:22; 61:12; 69:9; 65:11; 85:11; 98:8
557 Quran 56:34; 88:13
558 Quran 56:15
559 Quran 55:54
560 Quran 88:14-16
561 Quran 18:31; 22:23; 35:33; 76:21
562 Quran 18:31; 22:23; 35:33; 76:21; 46:53
563 Quran 18:31; 76:21
564 Quran 15:46; 18:31; 35:56; 37:44; 38:51; 52:20; 76:13; 82:23
565 Quran 15:47; 37:44; 44:53; 56:16
566 Quran 37:50; 52:25; 74:40
567 Quran 36:55
568 Quran 36:57; 38:51; 44:55
569 Quran 52:24; 56:17; 76:19
570 Quran 43:7
571 Quran 56:18
572 Quran 76:15
573 Quran 36:41
574 Quran 19:62
575 Quran 37:45; 52:23; 56:188; 76:17; 78:34; 83:25

576 Quran 52:22; 56:21
577 Quran 43:71
578 Quran 16:31; 39:34
579 Quran 50:35
580 Quran 9:72
581 Quran 2:217, 264, 266, 276; 3:22, 117; 5:5, 53; 7:147; 9:17, 52, 53-69; 14:18; 18:105; 24:39; 25:23; 33:19; 39:65; 47:9, 28, 32; 49:2
582 Quran 6:94; 11:21; 16:87; 28:75; 35:14; 40:74; 41:48; 46:28
583 Quran 29:23
584 Quran 4:137, 168; 47:34
585 Quran 83:15
586 Quran 2:174; 3:77
587 Quran 57:13
588 Quran 17:72, 97; 20:124
589 Quran 34:54
590 Quran 60:13
591 Quran 2:102; 3:77, 176; 42:20
592 Quran 7:51; 45:34
593 Quran 17:22
594 Quran 17:18, 39
595 Quran 42:8
596 Quran 7:40
597 Quran 16:84; 77:35, 36
598 Quran 6:21, 135; 10:17, 70; 16:117; 20:111; 23:117; 28:37; 91:10
599 Quran 2:27, 121; 3:85, 149; 4:119; 5:5, 52; 6:31, 140; 7:9, 53, 178; 9:69; 10:45-95; 11:21; 16:109; 22:11; 23:103; 29:52; 35:39; 39:15, 63, 65; 41:23, 25; 45:27; 46:18; 58:19; 63:9; 103:2
600 Quran 32:12; 42:45; 68:43; 70:44; 88:2
601 Quran 3:106; 39:60
602 Quran 75:24
603 Quran 10:27; 80:40, 41
604 Quran 3:30

605 Quran 18:49
606 Quran 24:24; 36:65; 41:20
607 Quran 6:31; 20:101
608 Quran 3:180
609 Quran 17:18, 22
610 Ibid, 39
611 Quran 40:10
612 Quran 6:124; 10:27; 16:27; 22:18; 25:69; 27:18; 40:60
613 Quran 11:18
614 Quran 69:25, 26, 27; 78:40
615 Quran 10:54; 21:97; 34:33
616 Quran 2:166
617 Quran 6:27; 26:102; 89:24
618 Quran 25:27-9
619 Quran 7:50; 78:24; 88:6,7
620 Quran 17:8
621 Quran 15:44
622 Quran 66:6; 74:30-1
623 Quran 4:145
624 Quran 90:20; 104:8
625 Quran 3:103
626 Quran 101:9, 11
627 Quran 25:12
628 Quran 67:7
629 Quran 77:32
630 Quran 25:13; 89:26
631 Quran 40:71; 69:32; 76:4
632 Quran 17:97; 25:34; 39:24
633 Quran 27:90
634 Quran 25:13
635 Quran 89:25
636 Quran 8:50; 22:9, 22; 85:10
637 Quran 2:24, 210; 11:98; 60:6; 72:15
638 Quran 22:21-2; 32:20
639 Quran 7:41; 18:29; 29:54-5; 39:16

640 Quran 14:50; 23:104; 33:66
641 Quran 70:16
642 Quran 74:29
643 Quran 104:7
644 Quran 9:35
645 Quran 23:107; 35:36; 40:49; 43:77
646 Quran 11:106; 21:100
647 Quran 4:56
648 Quran 40:71-72; 55:44
649 Quran 22:19, 20; 44:48
650 Quran 6:70; 10:4; 18:29; 37:67; 38:5; 47:15; 56:54-5; 78:25; 88:5
651 Quran 14:16-17; 69:36
652 Quran 37:66; 44:43-6; 56:52-3
653 Quran 73:12-3
654 Quran 56:42
655 Quran 56:43-4; 77:30
656 Quran 38:57-8; 78:25
657 Quran 88:3
658 Quran 3:191; 9:63; 11:60
659 Quran 38:4
660 Quran 43:67
661 Quran 7:38; 29:25
662 Quran 74:56
663 Quran 9:54
664 Quran 9:56
665 Quran 4:65
666 Muslim, *Sahih, 'Kitab al-Aqdiyya', Bab* 8
667 Muslim, *Sahih, 'Kitab al-Libas,' Bab* 10
668 See Abu Talib Al-Makki, *Qut al-qulub*, vol. 4, p. 33
669 E.g., Quran 2:62; 2:18; 17:19; 4:151
670 Quran 22:3; 49:3
671 Quran 26:89; 50:33
672 Quran 2:189
673 Quran 5:2

674 Muslim, *Sahih, 'Kitab al-Birr', Bab* 7
675 Al-Bukhari, *Sahih, 'Kitab al-Iman', Bab* 39
676 Quran 2:265
677 Quran 9:103
678 Quran 46:19
679 Quran 99:7-8
680 Al-Bukhari, *Sahih, 'Kitab al-Riqaq', Bab* 30; Muslim, *'Kitab al-Iman,' Bab* 57
681 Quran 4:95, 9:120-1
682 Cf. al-Bukhari, *Sahih,* first *hadith*
683 Ibid.
684 Ibid.
685 Quran 2:139; 7:29; 39:2, 11, 14; 40:14, 65; 98:5
686 Quran 4:135; 28:50; 38:26
687 Quran 4:108, 142; 5:54; 33:39
688 Quran 76:9
689 Quran 74:6
690 Quran 92:17-20
691 Quran 9:104
692 Malik, *al-Muwatta', 'Kitab al_Targhib fi'l-sadaqa', Bab* 1
693 Quran 2:272; 4:114; 20:14; 30:39
694 Quran 45:13
695 Quran 3:14; 40:39; 43:35
696 Quran 43:12-13
697 Quran 25:43-44
698 Quran 9:54, 98
699 Quran 2:237
700 Draz p. 211
701 Quran 4:75
702 Quran 2:193
703 A-Bukhari, *Sahih, 'Kitab al-Tawhid', Bab* 28
704 Quran 4:65
705 Malik, *al-Muwatta', 'Kitab al-Jihad, Bab* 1; al-Bukhari, *Sahih, 'Kitab al-Musaqat', Bab* 13; Muslim, *Sahih, 'Kitab al-Zakat', Bab* 6

706 Quran 5:3
707 Quran 2:153; 7:56
708 Ahmed, *Musnad*, vol. 5, p. 388
709 Quran 26:89
710 Al-Bukhari, *Sahih, 'Kitab al-Tahajjud'*, vol.6
711 See for example Quran 7:55, 56; 17:57; 39:9
712 Cf. *Al-Bukhari, Sahih, 'Kitab al-Zakat', Bab* 49
713 Cf. Muslim, *Sahih, 'Kitab al-Iman', Bab Kitab al-Kibr'*; Cf. al-Tirmidhi, *'Kitab al-Adab', Bab* 53
714 Ahmad, *Musnad*, vol. 2, p. 108
715 Quran 27:35; 2:75
716 Quran 2:231
717 Quran 4:12
718 Quran 68:17-33
719 Quran 4:29
720 Cf. Al-Bukhari, *Sahih, 'Kitab al-Iman', Bab 42*
721 Al-Bukhari, *Sahih, 'Kitab al-Ijara', Bab* 20
722 al_Bukhari, *Sahih, 'Kitab al-Libas', Bab* 7; Cj. Malik, *al-Muwatta, 'Kitab al-Salat al-Jum'a'*
723 Quran 107:6
724 Cf. Muslim, *Sahih, 'Kitab al-'Imara', Bab* 43
725 Ahmad, *Musnad*, vol. 5, p. 428-9
726 Al-Bukhari, *Sahih, 'Kitab al-Jihad', Bab* 15; Muslim, *Sahih, 'Kitab al-Imara', Bab* 42
727 Muslim, *Sahih, 'Kitab al-Zuhd', Bab* 5
728 Quran 9:102
729 Cf. Quran 16:78
730 Quran 91:7-8
731 Quran 91:9-10
732 Quran 9:105
733 Quran 84:6
734 Quran 64:16
735 Quran 90:11-17
736 Quran 26:69
737 Al-Bukhari, *Sahih, 'Kitab al-Riqaq', Bab* 37

738 Muslim, *Sahih, 'Kitab Sifat al-Qiyama'*
739 Quran 2:165
740 Cf. Bukhari, *Sahih, 'Kitab al-Adab', Bab* 33
741 Cf. al-Bukhari, *Sahih, 'Kitab al-Tawhid', Bab* 54. Muslim, *Sahih, 'Kitab al-Qadar', Bab* 1
742 Quran 92:5-10
743 Cf. Al-Tabarani, quoted by al-Suyuti, *al-Jami'*
744 Cf. Muslim, *Sahih, 'Kitab al-Qadar', Bab* 8
745 Quran 94:7-8
746 Quran 5:87-8
747 Muslim, *Sahih, 'Kitab al-Nikah', Bab* 1
748 Quran 62:10, 15
749 Quran 9:38-42; 9:81; 9:120
750 Quran 5:32
751 Cf. al-Tirmidhi, *Sunan, 'Kitab Sifat al-qiyama', Bab* 55
752 Quran 73:6
753 Cf. al-Bukhari, *Sahih, 'Kitab al-I'tikaf', B*ab 1
754 Quran 4:29
755 Quran 2:195
756 Cf. Al-Bukhari, *Sahih, 'Kitab al-'Umra', Bab* 58
757 Quran 6:119
758 Quran 5:3
759 Quran 2:184; 4;186; 42:43; 46:end
760 Cf. Bukhari, *Sahih, 'Kitab al-Adab', Bab* 84-6
761 Ahmad via Anas; Cf. al-Bukhari, *Sahih, 'Kitab al-Iman', Bab* 29
762 See for example Quran 3:102; 22:78
763 Cf. al-Tirmidhi, *'Kitab al-Sifat al-qiyama', Bab* 58
764 Quran 5:87; 7:31
765 Quran 23:5-7; 70:29-30
766 Quran 6:141; 17:29; 25:67
767 Quran 17:110; 31:19
768 Cf. al-Bukhari, *Sahih, 'Kitab al-Iman', Bab* 29